THE NINETIES

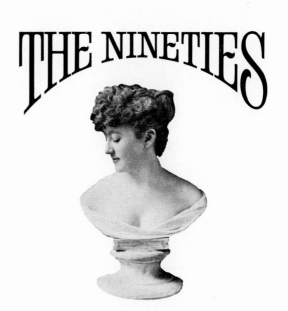

Glimpses of
a lost but lively world, by the
Editors of American Heritage

THE

Staff for this book

OLIVER JENSEN, *Editor in Charge*

MURRAY BELSKY, *Art Director*

DOUGLAS TUNSTELL, *Picture Editor*

Assisted by David McCullough,
Robert L. Reynolds, E. M. Halliday,
Joan Paterson Kerr, David G. Lowe,
Brenda Niemand, Suzanne A. Smith,
Robert Gallagher, Barbara Klaw,
Rosemary L. Klein, Arthur Korant

AMERICAN HERITAGE
The Magazine of History

James Parton, *President*

Joseph J. Thorndike, *Chairman,
      Editorial Committee*

Bruce Catton, *Senior Editor*

Oliver Jensen, *Editor*

Irwin Glusker, *Senior Art Director*

Darby Perry, *Publisher*

Our cover, as with any sensible book or magazine, is graced
by a Lady. We capitalize the word advisedly, for the Lady,
wasp-waisted, puff-shouldered, wrapped in enough garments to dress a dozen women of the 1960's, was one of the
most remarkable and romantic productions of the Mauve
Decade. This Lady, however, is not just another Gibson
Girl, waiting for a typical Gibson Man to return from bot-
tling up the Spanish Fleet and dart her a few hot glances;
she is the noted Mrs. Robert Sanderson McCormick, wife
of a diplomat who was variously minister to Austria, ambassador to Russia, and ambassador to France. Her father,
Joseph Medill (see page 26), published the Chicago *Tribune;* one of her sons, Colonel Robert R. "Bertie" McCormick, later became editor of the same paper; another,
Joseph Medill McCormick, married a daughter of Mark
Hanna and represented Illinois in the U.S. Senate. Quite a
different matter, alas! is the situation of the poor creature
on the back cover, which shows two deathless moments in a
very popular melodrama of the 90's. Struggling against The
Fate Worse Than Death was doubtless exhausting (especially before Freud had explained everything), but it was
perhaps more interesting than the sheltered life of a Lady.

COVER, COURTESY ART INSTITUTE OF CHICAGO, GIFT OF ESTATE OF COL. ROBERT
R. MCCORMICK; BACK COVER, CULVER; HALF TITLE PHOTO, MESERVE COLLECTION

2

NINETIES

CONTENTS

EDITOR'S INTRODUCTION 5

1890 *by W. A. Swanberg* 6

CHICAGO *by Robert S. Gallagher* 12

THE MAKING OF THE PRESIDENT, 1896 *by Stephen Hess* . . . 30

LIGHTS AND SHADOWS *A collection of photographs* 36

MORGAN TO THE RESCUE *by Andy Logan* 60

WHEN EVERYONE KNEW WHAT HE LIKED *by David G. Lowe* . 64

A NINETIES READER 80

A BOYHOOD IN THE NINETIES *by Gerard E. Jensen* . . . 90

INNOCENT MERRIMENT (MORE OR LESS)
                                    by Heywood Hale Broun . 97

A FLING AT EMPIRE 106

THE SPANISH FLEET COMES OUT TO DIE *by Walter Millis* . . 113

ON THE MAKING OF SPLENDID LITTLE WARS *by Ralph Andrist* . 117

HAPLESS HORATIO, THE GILDED HACK *by Robert S. Gallagher* . 120

THE NINETIES LOOK TO THE FUTURE *by H. G. Wells* . . 142

WHO CARES? *by Charles Dana Gibson* 144

Editor's Introduction

Some people thought them gay, some rather somber. To some who are still with us, the last ten years of the nineteenth century were the springtime of life. The land was full of sounds no longer heard: the hissing of lamps, the moans and shrieks of locomotive whistles, the clopping of horses' hoofs. It was a predominantly rural country, and most of its citizens were descended from the people of the British Isles, churchgoers, Chautauqua-goers, believers in a now-vanishing ethic. For all the overstuffed styles and busy decoration of the era, these were, by and large, happy people who thought that progress and civilization had attained almost dizzy heights and smiled particularly on America.

The decade of the 1890's marks a dividing line between that older, isolated America and the new urban society of our own times, the era of income taxes, big government, vast technology, restless minorities, and international horrors. In those years the frontier closed and the last Indian war parties faded away. Already the expanding and aggressive industries that had sprung up since the Civil War made a sign that rural America was passing. To man them, immigrants poured in from new lands and cultures, with profound effect on the future shape of the republic. We ventured forth beyond our continental limits to plant the flag in Hawaii, in the Philippines, and in the West Indies, and our isolation came to an end.

There is no going back in history, no Wellsian time machine to transport us magically back to the Mauve Decade, even if anyone who knows the present—for all its flaws—should want to return to days both kind and cruel, prosperous and bleak, fastidious and crude. But art and the historian can take us there to relive at least some of the era vicariously, and that is what we have undertaken in this book, which constitutes a kind of special, or extra, issue of AMERICAN HERITAGE Magazine. We hope we have cast on the Nineties as good a light, in as many colors, as might have shone from the old Tiffany lamps that face this page.

—Oliver Jensen

January 1, 1890 ... The New York *Tribune,* on the streets long before the last roisterers have vanished with the stars, hails the day with an editorial saying, "Rarely does a year begin with fairer promise of beneficence in all that concerns the National well-being." The philosopher-historian John Fiske is so impressed by the country's progress that he predicts a population of 600,-000,000 a century hence. The warm feeling of prosperity, of greatness, of optimism, of happy-New-Year and God-be-praised is so prevalent in the East as to suggest that there are few dissenting votes.

The dissenting votes exist, but they go uncounted in this rosy regional glow. They are beyond the horizon, out of hearing on this festive day, but they are there nevertheless. True, America's bigness, its bursting energy and enterprise, are rousing certainties. Across the land, men sweat at blast furnaces, run businesses, oversee endless acres, tend vast herds, go down into mines, put up new buildings. Yet despite her vigor, America's balance and solidarity are not altogether certain. The railroad and the telegraph span the land but have not yet conquered the provincialism that preceded them, and the failures in rapport can be astonishing. The differences are more than geographical, as can be seen in the surroundings and attitudes of two mythical but fairly representative couples who

It looked like a great decade coming up. Good things were busting out all over; anybody might find acres of diamonds. Had the millennium arrived? Well, not quite.

By W. A. SWANBERG

1890

might be named Jones and Brown. The Joneses, quite prosperous, live in New York City. The Browns, quite otherwise, live on a Kansas farm 1,300 miles west. Even if 1890 is technically the last year of the ninth decade, both couples feel that they are heading into the Nineties.

The Joneses' bedroom emphasizes tassels, curlicues, and dark oak furniture; their living room displays a group of horsehair-covered sofa and chairs blockaded and almost vanquished by decorative objects—bamboo jardinières, a stuffed owl, a sprawling easel displaying a chromolithograph, baroque stands bearing statuettes, a glass dome over wax flowers, vases of cattails, heavy portières. The new electric lights are in, covered by fringed shades, but many of the old gas jets are still working on a stand-by basis. The telephone, very hard on hearing but marvelous for all that, is fastened to the wall. Already the Manhattan directory has grown to be a thick pamphlet. The spacious bathroom has the three plumbing essentials, but only recently has the ghastly old zinc-lined bathtub been replaced by one enamelled with glistening white porcelain. The Joneses have a family physician, of course, but they also read advertisements and rely on certain "proven" patent medicines to quell minor disturbances. On the shelf is an array of bottles including Dr. Hostetter's Celebrated Stomach Bitters, almost half alcohol and certain to make one feel better in a crisis, and Lydia E. Pinkham's Vegetable Compound (eighteen per cent alcohol but all right with the temperance movement since it is not, on the surface, "liquor"), which Mrs. Jones sips for occasional female complaints.

Some of these complaints come from the clothing she wears. This armor is based on the steel-reinforced corset, drawn especially tight for gala affairs but worn every day in the year by women of decency and estimated to exert from twenty-one to eighty-eight pounds of pressure. Over this comes a succession of undergarments and petticoats topped by the external culmination, the dress with its bustle, an outjutting fraud made of padding that hugs the upper derrière and sharply contrasts the wasp waist with the bouffant folds below. Such a floor-sweeping costume requires at least fifteen yards of material.

Jones himself is relatively lucky in wearing a suit not drastically different from the style of three quarters of a century later, though surmounted by a high stiff collar that holds his neck rigid. He wears both beard and mustache, unmoved as yet by Charles Dana Gibson's drawings in *Life* of stunning young women and handsome, clean-shaven men that will soon start a trend against whiskers. The street outside is paved with asphalt, though cobblestones still rattle wagons in the business district. Jones goes to work in an elevated train drawn by a steam locomotive that scorches pedestrians and horses below with sparks; others use the cable cars or the few remaining horse cars.

The home is sacred, the husband is boss, and woman's place is in the background. The feminist outcries of Elizabeth Cady Stanton and Susan B. Anthony, considered merely amusing by many, are regarded by such influential clergymen as Dr. Morgan Dix as subversive efforts to lure woman away from her fireside. The coeducation practiced at Oberlin College and the University of Michigan is clearly immoral, and such women's schools as Vassar and Smith, while avoiding the mingling of the sexes, nevertheless indoctrinate young ladies with reprehensible thoughts of abandoning childrearing for careers of their own. The liquor interests, for once, are wholeheartedly with Dr. Dix, opposing woman suffrage because it might result in temperance legislation, and the southern delegation in Congress is as adamant, since votes for women might open the door to widespread voting by Negroes.

Jones votes Republican and marvels at American progress. He is impatient with visiting Britons like Herbert Spencer, who felt that Americans were too worshipful of the cash register, and the late Matthew Arnold, who also saw an enterprise so determined that it neglected "elevation and beauty." British lecturers are always enterprising enough to demand high American fees, are they not? Exactly a century ago George Washington was serving his first year as President of a nation of less than four million people. The United States, which before the Civil War stood fifth among manufacturing nations, now is running almost neck and neck with England for first place. What colossal growth! Let British critics ponder the fact that at the Paris Exposition in '89 Americans carried away 53 grand prizes, 199 gold medals, 271 silver medals, and 218 bronze medals. There is, Jones believes, *nothing* wrong with this country.

Here is where the Browns come in, sharply disagreeing, as do several million other voting farmers in the West and South. Ten years earlier the Browns took a 160-acre homestead in Kansas, built a sod house, and made the prairie bloom with corn. On the strength of one bumper crop they abandoned the smelly sod hut and risked a mortgage to build a four-room frame house. They bought a cow by borrowing from the bank. They have never been able to retire these debts. Even when crops are good, the twenty-eight cents a bushel they get for their corn leaves no margin. They never go hungry, and there is an inspirational quality in life next to the soil that the Joneses will never feel, but with it goes a foreboding that they are losing ground in a day-by-day struggle for solvency. Supposing sickness comes this year, or a poor crop? They know their mortgage will be foreclosed; it happened to two of their nearest neighbors a mile away last year. It is as well that they do not know that in the next four years there will be more

ALL: SY SEIDMAN

Negroes, said Booker T. Washington, sizing up the 90's attitude, must begin "at the bottom of life," work up slowly.

When Jacob S. Coxey's "army" of unemployed marched to Washington, their commander wound up in jail for trespassing on the Capitol's grass.

Feminist bigwigs like these were a formidable lot. "Call on God; She will help you," one is said to have enjoined.

than eleven thousand farm mortgage foreclosures in the state of Kansas alone.

They light kerosene lamps this morning with none of the jauntiness of the Joneses. They work hard seven days a week, Mrs. Brown caring for the cow and chickens as well as for the children. Their house has only homemade furniture, the barest necessities, with a privy sixty feet south of the kitchen door. Mrs. Brown uses her one worn corset only for church meetings and socials. Brown's lone Sunday suit, bought in 1883, is baggy and patched, and the children are not quite but almost ragged. The Browns think that free silver will solve their problems. Naturally they listen to spokesmen who understand them—Sockless Jerry Simpson, broke himself, who blames it on the railroads, bankers, and grain gamblers; and fiery Mary Lease, who urges the farmers to "raise less corn and more hell." At political meetings they sing:

> *The railroads and old party bosses*
> *Together did sweetly agree;*
> *And they thought there would be little trouble*
> *In working a hayseed like me.*

The Browns have not yet heard of thirty-year-old, trombone-voiced William Jennings Bryan, who is preparing to run for Congress over in Nebraska, imbued with the feeling he finds all around him that the railroads, banks, and monopolies are squeezing the farmer dry. In South Carolina a one-eyed farmer named Ben Tillman was doing passably until "the devil tempted me to buy a steam engine and other machinery . . . all on credit." A crop failure all but ruined him and now he is on the political warpath. In Indiana young Eugene Debs is beseeching the various squabbling railroad brotherhoods to merge into one powerful union that can bargain for better wages and working conditions. In California farmers are so enraged at the ruthless landlordship and monopolistic rates of the Southern Pacific that they make folk heroes of two gunmen named Chris Evans and John Sontag, whose specialty is plugging S.P. agents and robbing express cars.

In 1890, while Americans congratulate themselves on the end of sectionalism, a new sectionalism is rising. The old grudge is about over, the bloody shirt worn to a mere thread. Sherman is the only leading Union general still living, Lee is long gone, and Jeff Davis died in 1889. Thousands of Union and Confederate veterans assembled at Gettysburg in almost tearful harmony in 1888 to celebrate the twenty-fifth anniversary of their unfriendly encounter there. Confederates, of course, get no federal pensions, but the old blues get them and the G.A.R. is asking for more, to the distress of Mr. Jones. The tariff yields a surplus—truly, a big annual government surplus—and part of it goes not only to veterans and their dependents but to fringe beneficiaries who never fired a bullet.

The new 1890 sectionalism is economic, and who is interested in economics except when it bites? Roughly the split is between the heartland area east of the Mississippi and north of the Ohio-Potomac line, and the rest of the country, the outland; between urban and rural elements; between business and industry on one hand and agriculture on the other. The nation, revering individual independence, is traditionally opposed to vesting more power in Washington, but since the war such independence has become nearly impossible. The westerners and southerners are entirely dependent on railroads, bankers, the price they pay for necessities, and the price they get for their produce, none of which they can control. The every-man-for-himself spirit, so admirable a half century earlier, is passé in 1890. The nation has outgrown its government, which is still—except for a tariff beneficial to manufacturers—largely on a *laissez faire, caveat emptor* basis, and the shrewd ones are exploiting the *emptor*. The financial and industrial elements profiting from *laissez faire* are perfectly happy with it, but discontent stalks the agriculturists caught in the squeeze.

The idea that change is needed is hard for the snug Joneses to grasp. Is not the whole point about America its freedom and equal opportunity for all? There is a push and hurry seen in no other country. F. W. Woolworth is slaving sixteen hours a day to increase his growing chain of five-and-dime stores. The books of Horatio Alger demonstrate the easy steps by which a poor but honest young man can ascend to honorable wealth. The Philadelphia clergyman Russell Conwell has already delivered his famous "Acres of Diamonds" lecture more than 3,000 times, explaining "how men and women may become rich," describing the pursuit of wealth as a duty shirked only by the lazy: "I say, get rich, get rich! But get money honestly or it will be a withering curse." Some are willing to risk the curse. Henry James has fled the barbarism of money-getting America, and Charles Francis Adams is so disillusioned by the cultural destitution of business leaders he has met that he says, "Not one that I have ever known would I care to meet again, either in this world or the next...."

But surely Adams said this in a dyspeptic moment, for things are looking up. The self-made pushers are being joined by a growing stream of college-trained men who intermix music, art, or social conscience with their more expedient aspirations. President Harrison himself is a graduate of Miami University, and such college-bred leaders as Theodore Roosevelt, Abram Hewitt, William C. Whitney, and Henry Cabot Lodge are anything but single-track drones. Brilliant immigrants like Joseph Pulitzer and Carl Schurz spread intellectuality along with reform. New York's Metropolitan Opera is thriving (the Joneses admire the "boy wonder" conductor, Walter Damrosch). The New York Philharmonic Orchestra and the Boston Symphony are long established; in 1891 Theodore Thomas will start conducting the Chicago Symphony; and serious playgoers can enjoy splendid performances by Edwin Booth, Joseph Jefferson, or Richard Mansfield. Although many readers feel that there is no real American literature and prefer English novels—*Black Beauty* is one that swamps the country in tears in 1890—others are coming around to see Mark Twain as an artist rather than a crude jokester, and William Dean Howells has his partisans. *Scribner's, Harper's Monthly,* and *Century* are magazines catering to the intellectuals. Such colorists as Winslow Homer and Thomas Eakins have brought back from Europe a new virility in painting, and Saint-Gaudens and MacMonnies show the same spirit in sculpture.

If this is a cultural wasteland, its oases are growing. For the lower-browed, every middling town has its opera house, a dozen companies of minstrels tour the country, and John L. Sullivan himself plays Simon Legree in one of the many *Uncle Tom's Cabin* troupes still riding the rails. *East Lynne* and *Bertha, the Sewing Machine Girl* draw packed houses, while in Deadwood, South Dakota, Calamity Jane grows so indignant at a stage villain that she spits a long, accurate jet of tobacco juice to give him his comeuppance. The lovely Liza in *The White Slave* draws cheers when she declaims, "Rags are royal raiment when worn for virtue's sake." The piano is everywhere, even in Colorado miners' shacks, and favorite numbers range from the sentimental "Always Take Mother's Advice" to the uproarious "Throw Him Down, McCloskey." The national yearning for enlightenment brings thousands in person to the great Chautauqua Assembly in upstate New York, and many more thousands take its extension courses, while smaller, imitation Chautauquas bloom elsewhere. The *Ladies' Home Journal* has reached a circulation of over 500,000. Its editor, twenty-seven-year-old Edward Bok, is embarrassed when he urges young women to address their problems to Ruth Ashmore, who is really Bok, and finds them querying him about romance and even sex. If dime novels are frowned on, they at least require an ability to

Homestead, Pennsylvania, 1892: spectators await developments in one of the nation's bloodiest strikes, at the big plant of the Carnegie Steel Company.

Emma Goldman and Alexander Berkman, anarchists, plotted to assassinate Carnegie's lieutenant, H. C. Frick, but bungled it. Berkman got fourteen years.

Harper's Weekly, JULY 14, 1894

Eugene Debs' leadership of the Pullman strike of 1894 won him a tin crown from Harper's Weekly—and six months in jail.

The horseless carriage led a host of engineering wonders. In 1895, Charles E. Duryea's model (above) was the fastest.

Techniques of bridgebuilding, when applied to corset design, achieved a breath-taking contrast between bust and waist.

For only $9.95 Sears, Roebuck would let you walk your baby in this super-Victorian carriage. Rubber tires 75¢ extra.

read, and one purveyor of them, Erastus F. Beadle, is already a millionaire.

Through lyceum circuits people in the provinces can hear Bill Nye crack jokes, John Stoddard give travel talks about far places, illustrated with stereopticon slides, and—Russell Conwell repeat once more his "Acres of Diamonds." In summer there is baseball and croquet; in the fall college football is ferocious; and what can compare with the circuses, some forty of which are on tour, including the mammoth combined Barnum and Bailey show? Things are popping—new sensations, new inventions, new headliners.

The fact remains that the Joneses and the Browns, financially and culturally, live in different worlds. The Joneses, enjoying the best in music and the drama, can discuss the fine points of John Drew's Petruchio and Ada Rehan's Kate in Broadway's current *Taming of the Shrew*. The Browns, by the most stringent penny-pinching, manage a once-a-year spree, getting the children to town for a circus in the afternoon and a melodrama in the evening. But both families read the newspapers and are amazed by the globe-girdling speed of the petite New York *World* reporter Nellie Bly. She left New York last November 14 with the absurd idea of beating the eighty-day record of Jules Verne's fictional Phileas Fogg, using only conventional modes of transportation. The *World* cannily whips up excitement with daily reports of her progress and cabled dispatches from Miss Bly. She stops in Amiens to interview Monsieur Verne, who laughs indulgently and says she will never make it. Brindisi . . . Aden . . . Colombo . . . Singapore . . . Hong Kong . . . it actually appears that she will. She sails from Yokohama January 7 and reaches San Francisco on the twenty-first.

When she arrives in New York January 25, having travelled 24,899 miles in less than seventy-three days, cannon boom at the Battery and thousands cheer the intrepid girl in the checked suit. "FATHER TIME OUTDONE!" headlines the *World*; "Even Imagination's Record Pales Before the Performance of the *World*'s Globe-Circler." Although this is clearly another of the many circulation stunts contrived by Joseph Pulitzer's newspaper, there is no denying that it is an American triumph that makes travel seem easy and shrinks the world to ridiculously small proportions.

America in 1890 is a wonderful place to live, except for that growing imbalance. Millionaires have become such common phenomena that the New York *Tribune* will soon count them and discover 4,047 in the country, of whom 145 are in San Francisco, 280 in Chicago, and 1,103 in New York (not counting 155 in the separate city of Brooklyn). There are none in Kansas. Since there is virtually no government supervision of trade and speculation, the prevailing practice of big business is not technically illegal but very sharp and ruthless, following the pattern of success set by the Vanderbilts, Rockefeller, and Gould.

Thus the charming and able William C. Whitney, lately Cleveland's Secretary of the Navy, got his fingers burned in a railroad deal with William H. Vanderbilt and Andrew Carnegie, but learned so much strategy in the encounter that he will soon make $40,000,000 in water-soaked traction manipulations and other enterprises. Whitney smilingly explains to his pastor, the Reverend William S. Rainsford, why he is dropping James Carter as his attorney in favor of Elihu Root: "Carter tells me what I cannot do, and Root what I can." Young James "Buck" Duke, who rose from poverty in North Carolina, is now in New York, manufacturing cigarettes by the carload despite pulpit warnings that the weed will drive people insane. Duke, ignorant except in business, aims to do in tobacco what Rockefeller did in oil. "First," Duke says, "you hit your enemies in the pocketbook, hit 'em hard. Then you either buy 'em out or take 'em in with you." Duke hits 'em so hard that he is on the road to amassing nearly $100,000,000.

With no income tax, the problem of spending large fortunes can be considerable. New mansions are springing up on Fifth Avenue—there are three at the corner of Fifty-seventh Street alone, each worth more than a half million—and the Vanderbilts, Astors, Belmonts, and many others are bringing over European paintings and statuary by the boatload. In fierce competition for glitter, the wealthy build summer palaces at Newport, acquire crown jewels, buy strings of race horses and long yachts with crews of forty or more dressed in the owner's colors—they even buy gem-studded collars for dogs. But not even a one-hundred-foot ballroom can hold all the rich, and Ward McAllister is making a career of snobbery, telling Mrs. William Astor whom she can safely exclude and saying that only four hundred people really count in New York society anyway.

The Joneses deplore the vulgarity of this excess but accept it as proof of an expanding economy. The Browns in Kansas read about it first with unbelief, then with what might in understatement be called rising indignation.

The Senate has its own rich men's club, with such moneybags as the railroad mogul Stanford of California, the capitalist Aldrich of Rhode Island, the lawyer-promoter Payne of Ohio, the mining millionaire George Hearst of California, the railroad and canal tycoon Gorman of Maryland, and the lumber baron Sawyer of Wisconsin. These self-made men and others around them believe in business and industry as the root of prosperity and are unsympathetic with bucolic complaint. Easterners in general recall the bloody Haymarket Riot in Chicago in 1886, which the newspapers laid to anarchists, and tend to agree that westerners are violent and somewhat lawless people, gripped by a six-shooter mentality and susceptible to revolutionary talk imported from Europe. Haymarket has given the whole labor movement a bad name, so that the strikes of 1890 are often viewed as subversive rather than as signs of a need for reform.

In the summer the Joneses, members of the Murray Hill Cycling Club, bicycle with their friends on Sundays along Riverside Drive. There is a civic fuss about this, one group being in stern opposition on two counts: such pleasure is sinful on the Sabbath, and the sport is clearly not for ladies. The critics are losing ground fast. Sunday is the only free day, a day when blue laws have closed the museums, concert halls, baseball parks, and even the saloons; and besides, cycling is ripping good fun. The new safety bicycle with equal-sized wheels and cushioned rubber tires can attain an exhilarating fifteen miles an hour even when propelled by an amateur. The drop-frame women's bike allows the skirt to veil most of the legs, and while there is regrettably a portion of ankle revealed on the downstroke, this problem is solved (though not to the satisfaction of the conservatives) by the wearing of high gaiters. But bicycling is still an urban sport, dependent on smooth macadam, impossible for the Browns in Kansas even if they could afford a wheel. When the Browns go to town, they hitch a draft horse to their only wagon, made of rough planks.

New York's Madison Square Garden, designed by Stanford White, is now under construction. The largest hall in the world, with 10,000 seats, it will sponsor bicycle races as well as many other events. The scandal of the new Garden is Saint-Gaudens' lovely gold Diana topping the tower, naked to the waist as she draws her bow. Clergymen erupt in protest, and one opportunist does a brisk business renting binoculars to curious men on the square below. But J. P. Morgan, the biggest stockholder in the Garden, holds his ground, Diana holds hers, and puritanism takes another setback.

The expansion of government is as slow and reluctant as the decline of prudery. But 1890 sees a social landmark in the federal move against monopolies. The archetype is Standard Oil, which under John D. Rockefeller has achieved such efficiency in the extermination of competitors as to enjoy a virtual monopoly both in oil and in public disapproval. The Joneses regard Rockefeller as the genius of American enterprise, who deserves all the rewards of his marvelous efficiency and foresight. It is with misgivings that they admit he may need a trifle of

CONTINUED ON PAGE 127

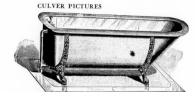

CULVER PICTURES

If you could afford a bathtub at all, you could afford one big enough, almost, to swim in. And look at those legs!

The garrulity of women on the rapidly multiplying telephones made many long-suffering men ask if God had not, for once, over-wrought.

The Wright brothers were still building bicycles when Samuel P. Langley's steam-powered but unmanned airplane, a true pioneer, flew successfully above the Potomac River in May, 1896.

ALL NATIONS ARE WELCOME TO THE WORLD'S COLUMBIA

CHICAGO

Hog butcher, city of the big shoulders
—in Sandburg's words—always
building, breaking, then rebuilding;
now this giant of the plains symbolized
to the world the American colossus

By ROBERT S. GALLAGHER

Uncle Sam extends his hand in welcome (left), but the expansive, almost arrogant, gesture of the lithographed invitation belongs to Chicago, flexing its rambunctious muscle before the nation and the world. On October 9, the twenty-second anniversary of the great fire, more than 760,000 citizens flocked to the Fair, some on the trolley roofs (below). Appropriately, most of the exposition's buildings burned shortly after it closed a few weeks later.

The phenomenal growth of Chicago after the Civil War had by the Nineties made it the first typically American metropolis—rail hub, manufacturing complex, great market place for the products of the farm; if the nation's cultural center of gravity still lay far to the east, the hustling city on Lake Michigan had intellectual pretensions of its own. Vulgar, materialistic, and aggressive it may have been, but Chicago in the Nineties was the loud-mouthed symbol of America. When a site was sought for an international exposition to mark the four-hundredth anniversary of Columbus' discovery, Chicago made the winning bid (backing it with a $5,000,-000 down payment), and quickly transformed some 600 acres of lake-front swamp into a glittering White City

13

of classical and Renaissance buildings, shimmering lagoons, and warbling gondoliers. Seventy-seven nations —a "paradise of ethnology"—participated in the Fair; Little Egypt introduced the *Danse du Ventre* at one exhibit, though more people paid to see Buffalo Bill at the nearby Coliseum; George Washington Ferris erected a huge wheel, a big favorite of the more than 27,000,000 visitors. But the main attraction, as travellers from everywhere discovered, was Chicago itself.

Wheat, pork, and iron made Chicago important; the railroads gave it power; profiteering during the Civil War and an unending flow of cheap immigrant labor made it rich. A blanket of industrial smog hung constantly over its more than 165 squat square miles, though not thickly enough to hide the continual manipulation and corruption of its politicians, one of

whom even insisted that the smoke was beneficial to children's lungs. The city's population—less than 30,000 when the railroad boom began in 1851—had passed one million by the opening of the Fair; seventy per cent were foreign-born, and their presence made of the city a colorful tapestry of nationalities that rivalled the international exhibits at the exposition.

Nor were any of the struggles and problems common to the nation as a whole in the Nineties missing in Chicago. Sectional antagonisms merely fired the energy of this restless city where eastern industrial drive meshed with frontier vitality. Immense wealth shared the sidewalks with abject poverty; capitalism rode rampant, ignoring the nascent labor movement in its midst; it was but a short ride from Chicago's theatres, libraries, and churches to its brothels, gambling dens,

14

Richard M. Hunt's French Renaissance administration building (left), with its 220-foot-high dome, dominated the exposition grounds, just as the neoclassic style of architecture would reign supreme in this country for half a century after the Fair. Chicagoans can still enjoy a promenade along Lake Michigan in Jackson Park (above), part of the planning legacy of Daniel Hudson Burnham (shown in caricature at right), who headed the famed team of architects and artists assembled to design the 1893 exposition.

and saloons. The fire of 1871 was only its most extensive, and Chicago treated such devastations as if they were heaven-sent urban renewal programs. Fifteen years later, a bomb went off in the Haymarket, and John Peter Altgeld stood for hours on a cold, drab, November afternoon watching the funeral cortege of four of the anarchists executed for throwing it. In 1893 Governor Altgeld ruined his career by pardoning the men convicted of the bombing.

All this and more Chicago took in its mighty stride; conflict had been part of its nature, its heritage; build, break, rebuild: this was the formula of greatness. "Chicago has chosen a star," Mayor Carter H. Harrison proudly proclaimed two days before the Fair closed. That night, the portly, sixty-nine-year-old mayor was assassinated by a demented office seeker.

Chicago's dependence on rail and water transportation is apparent in this artist's aerial conception of the city near the end of the century. The concentration of river-front warehouses and dock facilities attests to the city's historic use of the meandering "Checagou" River to ship in raw materials and carry out the finished products to the world's markets. The river had also been used as an open sewer and was the cause of periodic epidemics until

the direction of the flow was reversed from east to west after the Civil War by the deepening of the canal linking it with the Mississippi. Chicago's later and continuing reliance on the railroads is demonstrated by the numerous rail beds that penetrate its commercial district. The elevated railroad tracks of the city's now famous Loop district enclose the area bordered by Wabash and Fifth avenues and Van Buren and Lake streets.

The hustle and bustle of Chicago was everywhere apparent, from its congested waterways (above, the river at the Rush Street bridge) to its crowded commercial district, pictured at right in a view looking east on Madison Street. Below: The unique elevated system that circumscribes the Loop was completed in 1897.

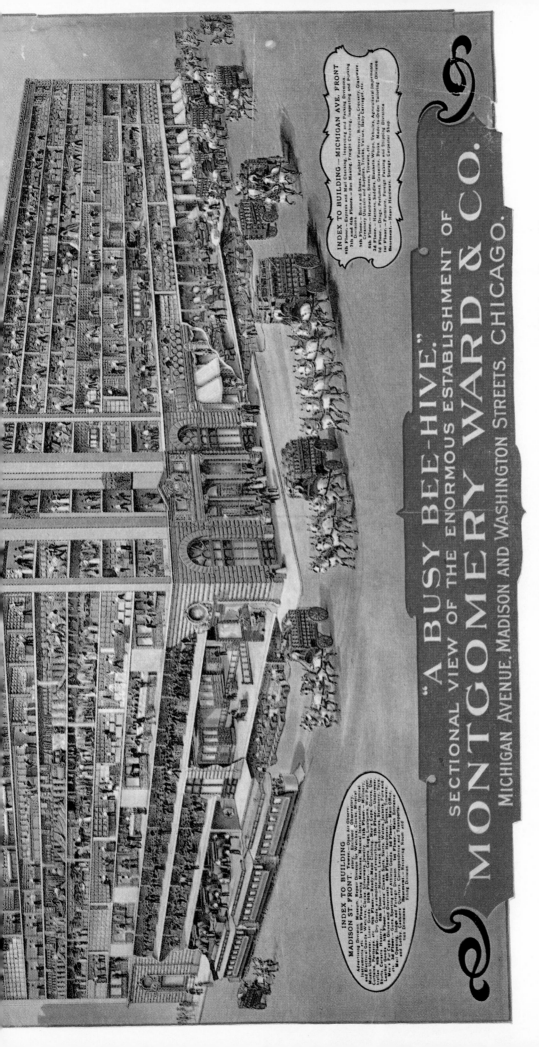

INDEX TO BUILDING — MICHIGAN AVE. FRONT

5th Floor.— Express and Mail Checking, Inspecting and Packing Divisions.
7th and 6th Floors.— Box Making, Freight Checking, Inspecting and Packing Divisions.
5th Floor.— Boot and Shoes, Rubber Footwear, Bicycles, Crockery, Glassware, Groceries, Utensils and Supplies, Trunks, Valises, Baby Carriages, etc.
4th Floor.— Hardware, Stoves, Tinware, etc.
3d Floor.— Harness, Saddles, Blankets, Whips, Vehicles, Agricultural Implements.
2d Floor.— Drugs, Perfumes, Groceries, Basket Made-to-Order Tailoring Division.
1st Floor.— Furniture, Furnace and Stove Packing and Shipping Divisions.
Basement.— Heavy Hardware, Storage, Carpenter Shop

"A BUSY BEE-HIVE."
SECTIONAL VIEW OF THE ENORMOUS ESTABLISHMENT OF
MONTGOMERY WARD & CO.
MICHIGAN AVENUE, MADISON AND WASHINGTON STREETS, CHICAGO.

INDEX TO BUILDING
MADISON ST. FRONT

Tower.— Open Air Observatory.
5th Floor.— Repair Division.
5th Floor.— Sewing Machines, Musical Instruments, Optical Goods, Watches, Clocks, Silverware.
6th Floor.— Draperies, Wall Paper, Carpets, Rugs, Linoleums, Wall Paper, etc.
5th Floor.— Complete line of everything. Under-wear, Corsets, Hosiery, Notions, Linens, Laces, Embroideries.
4th Floor.— Hardware, Cutlery, Sporting Goods, Jewelry, Ribbons, Silks, Dress Goods, Upholstery.
1st Floor.— Main Entrance, Mail Opening, Index and Forder Division.
Filing Division.

Busy, indeed! Chicago not only bought the farmer's wheat and the rancher's beef—it sold: everything and anything, anywhere, a yard of gingham, a billiard table, reaping machines, railroad cars. But then trading was the city's manifest destiny. From the earliest days, when French explorers bartered for furs with the Indians, Chicago was primarily a market place, first for the frontier, later for the middle border, finally for the nation. Many of its first millionaires made their fortunes in dry goods. Potter Palmer, for instance, sold partnerships in his retail enterprise to Marshall Field and Levi Z. Leiter, then after the

1871 fire built them a commercial palace (the weekly rent was an incredible $1,000) a few doors from his lavish Palmer House hostelry on State Street. About the same time, Montgomery Ward began exporting the wonders of the urban department store to the countryside; a regiment of fast-talking "drummers" was soon riding every railroad and stage from coast to coast. The company did not move into its "bee-hive" until 1899, by which time "Monkey Ward's" mail-order primacy was being successfully challenged by Sears, Roebuck and Company ("You Take No Risk"), with its revolutionary new annual catalogues.

The industrial inferno above—the name Dante often cropped up in conversations about the city's pollution problems—was the result of a molten mixture of Lake Superior ore and southern Illinois coal; by the 1890's, Chicago still lacked a giant steel corporation, but the many, many smelting firms in and around the city together annually outproduced Pittsburgh. Fortunately, most of the city's industry and its pungent stockyards (left) were undamaged by the 1871 fire, a fact that contributed greatly to the city's fantastic recovery. The human fuel for this gigantic industrial complex came in the form of immigrants, many of whom eventually made their way into working-class housing built near the factories, similar to the homes at right in the Maxwell Street area around 1900.

For the vast majority of Chicagoans in the city's sprawling slums, mere survival was a challenge. There the ethnic panorama was delineated on the signboards of neighborhood stores such as the German grocery above. Prices were extremely low (bread two cents a loaf), and so were wages, for long hours under primitive conditions. Photographer Sigmund Krausz focussed on the city's street types and produced a revealing record of the times (opposite), from the pathetic young match and flypaper salesman to the scissors sharpener, from the "Hallelujah-Lasses" to the city slicker preparing his advance on some Sister Carrie.

Mayor Carter H. Harrison (father) *Mayor Carter H. Harrison (son)*

Above: *Joseph Medill, publisher of the* Daily Tribune, *with grandchildren (clockwise) Robert R. McCormick, Eleanor Patterson, Joseph M. Patterson, Medill McCormick* **Right:** *Mrs. Potter Palmer, by A. Zorn* **Below:** *George Pullman and his family*

For years the East had haughtily dismissed Chicago as a smoky slaughterhouse devoted to "cash, cussing, and cuspidors." But by the Nineties, the city had become self-conscious about its cultural life, its three universities, its twenty-four theatres, and the symphony orchestra under Theodore Thomas' baton, which had rendered Bach and Beethoven for the construction workers at the Fair to put them in a proper mood to build classical structures. Two dozen daily newspapers served up the events of the universe to the residents of America's second largest metropolis, and, in addition, several hundred weekly, monthly, and quarterly magazines were published in the city.

The wives and daughters of its merchant princes travelled frequently to Europe, returning to hold court in opulent mansions along Lake Michigan. The most unusual of these monuments to affluence was the fantastic Gothic castle that Potter Palmer built on Lake Shore Drive in 1882. Here, amid untold treasures of art (an interior view appears on page 64), Mrs. Palmer posed for a somewhat romanticized portrait by Anders Zorn (right) and ruled a local society composed mainly of the city's commercial elite—McCormicks, Armours, Ryersons, Swifts, Fields, Searses, Deerings, Wards, and Wrigleys.

In the family of Joseph Medill, millionaire publisher of the Chicago *Daily Tribune,* the tradition of public service became a legend in the third generation: Robert R. McCormick took over the *Tribune;* Joseph Medill Patterson founded the New York *Daily News;* Eleanor "Cissy" Patterson was the publisher of the Washington *Times-Herald;* and Medill McCormick represented Illinois in the United States Senate. George Pullman, on the other hand, was viewed by his fellow industrialists as something of a Utopian when he constructed his model village in South Side Chicago for his workers. The members of Eugene V. Debs's American Railway Union had a different opinion and, after Pullman had slashed wages but not rents during the depression of 1893, a bloody strike ensued the following spring.

Violence, of course, is part of Chicago's history, dating back, some people insist, to 1812, when the Potawatomis destroyed Fort Dearborn. When the son and namesake of the murdered Mayor Carter H. Harrison was himself elected mayor in 1897, Finley Peter Dunne's Mr. Dooley insisted to a friend that Harrison couldn't be running for office because he had been assassinated almost four years before. "Was he?" the friend replied. "Ah, well, he's lived that down be this time. He was a good man."

Chicago swells mingled with bookies, touts, shillabers, and jams of tarts at Washington Park each year for the running of the Derby. The race was first held at the sumptuous racing club in 1884, and for years the city's society leaders paraded to the park in their polished victorias and landaus, which were prominently displayed at favored locations near the finish line. By the end of the decade, racing enthusiasts were treated to the spectacle of a tallyho filled with the lovely inhabitants of the Everleigh Club (right); the city's most renowned soiled doves, they received their customers in one of the lushest drawing rooms of the era. The 1893 Derby, which Theodore Groll captured in oil, was witnessed by hundreds of foreign visitors to the Columbian Exposition (Ferris' wheel dominates the distant Fair, seen in the right background).

28

Puck, JUNE 24, 1896

Puck portrayed McKinley's "coronation" by the GOP convention as having been managed by Hanna, Kohlsaat, and Ohio Congressman C. F.

HANNA: You can get both New York and Pennsylvania, Governor, but there are certain conditions.

MCKINLEY: What are they?

HANNA: They want a promise that you will appoint Tom Platt Secretary of the Treasury, and they want it in writing.

(Pause)

MCKINLEY: I can't do it, Mark.

THE MAKING

osvenor and showed the defeated "favorite sons" paying homage.

By STEPHEN HESS

As he ripped off the last leaf of the calendar, exposing the new year 1895, Marcus Alonzo Hanna turned his back on the business that bore his name, handed the keys to his younger brother Leonard, and, at the age of fifty-seven, began a new career whose purpose was to make William McKinley President of the United States.

It was hardly surprising that McKinley—"the Major," to his friends—aspired to the Presidency. He was midway in his second term as governor of Ohio. And Ohio, as James G. Blaine pointed out, "has always had its candidate." Grant had been born there, Hayes had been its chief executive, and Garfield had served it in the Congress. Moreover, the little Major—war hero, small-town lawyer, conscientious congressman—was the stuff of which American Presidents had been molded since Virginia lost its monopoly.

The aspirant President-maker, on the other hand, was a type rarely found in a political caucus. Hanna was a semi-self-made businessman who had taken his father-in-law's successful firm, Rhodes & Company, and turned it into the grossly successful M. A. Hanna & Company, employer of six thousand, dealer in coal, iron ore, and pig iron. As a hobby, Hanna owned all or part of the Globe Shipbuilding Company, the Cleveland City Railway Company (known as "Little Consolidated"), the Union National Bank of Cleveland, the Euclid Avenue Opera House, and for a short and unprofitable period, the Cleveland *Herald*. In an era when big businessmen shuffled and dealt politicos at will, it was almost unseemly for a man with a personal fortune in excess of seven million dollars to wish to exchange the countinghouse for the smoke-filled room. Certainly such a move would never have entered the mind of Hanna's childhood friend John D. Rockefeller.

McKinley and Hanna first met during the early 1870's. In 1876 McKinley defended a group of Hanna's striking coal miners who had been imprisoned for riot. The Canton lawyer won twenty-two out of twenty-three

OF THE PRESIDENT, 1896

Puck feared that the Populist-endorsed Bryan was gobbling up the Democratic party. Leading Populists held exactly the opposite opinion: "The Democratic idea of fusion," said one angrily, "is that we play Jonah while they play whale."

cases. The idea of making him President, however, did not occur to the Cleveland industrialist until they served together as delegates to the Republican National Convention of 1888.

The passage of the McKinley Tariff Act of 1890, a measure so inclusive that it protected even nonexistent American industries, resulted in the involuntary return to private life of a great many Republican congressmen, including the High Priest of Protection, William McKinley.

The resilient ex-congressman was elected governor in 1891. And at the 1892 presidential convention in broiling Minneapolis, when the delegates would have loved an excuse to retire their icy standard-bearer, President Benjamin Harrison, they began to flirt shamelessly with McKinley, who craftily ducked the dubious honor. After Harrison had been renominated, Hanna and McKinley adjourned to the hotel room of Herman H. Kohlsaat, a Chicago baker turned newspaper publisher; there, hot and exhausted, the three men stripped to their underwear and lay down on their beds. For a long while there was silence; then Hanna finally said,

"My God, William, that was a damned close squeak!"

Hanna was right: 1892 was not the year for an ambitious Republican to be running for the Presidency. On election night in Columbus, McKinley's young secretary watched McKinley watch Harrison lose to Grover Cleveland—"Everybody but the Governor lost his spirits, and he continued to smile until the final news came...." The smiling governor was re-elected the next year by some 80,000 votes, the largest plurality in Ohio since the Civil War. He made a mildly good chief executive, building a useful pro-labor record. But under the Ohio constitution a governor didn't have a great deal to do, which made the office a particularly bouncy springboard for higher office. During the off-year elections of 1894, when Republicans could only look up, Governor McKinley felt free to barnstorm the country—north to St. Paul, south to New Orleans, east to Maine. He travelled twelve thousand miles, speaking 371 times to two million people in sixteen states. In Kansas he made thirteen speeches in one day; Republican Committeeman Joseph L. Bristow described their stop at Scranton, a coal-mining town:

The miners had come out of the mines and gathered around the rear end of the car, many with the lamps burning in their caps, and their faces begrimed with coal dust. McKinley talked to them in a conversational tone on the tariff. . . . He spoke in a fatherly and sympathetic way, and tears gathered in the eyes and rolled down the faces of many of those who stood near him. To make men weep in discussing the tariff deeply impressed me. . . .

(As a result of this trip, Bristow said later, all the Kansas delegates were pledged to McKinley in 1896, "and not a dollar of campaign funds was sent into the state by Mr. Hanna.") On McKinley's return home, Hanna supposedly told him, "I thought you would be dead," and the Major replied, "From the itinerary you gave me I thought your purpose was to kill me."

As befitted a newly retired millionaire, Hanna rented a large winter house in the resort town of Thomasville, near Georgia's southern border. There, for three weeks in March of 1895, he entertained the Ohio governor and his wife. McKinley called the visit just "a little rest and outing." Yet on his arrival Hanna's sun parlor began filling with key southern Republicans. They were a notoriously venal lot, who, one of them admitted, viewed presidential conventions "as a kind of hog-killing time." While their support in the solidly Democratic South would be worthless in November, at conventions campaign managers viewed them as things of beauty. The states of the old Confederacy would hold 222 votes at the 1896 Republican convention, nearly half of the number necessary for a nomination, and all but twenty-six would go to McKinley. Hanna probably made no outright purchases, but as he wrote Carnegie's lawyer, Philander C. Knox, ". . . we have to pay travelling expenses to most of the delegates to the Convention."

Later in 1895 Hanna went to New York to meet with Tom Platt, the state's "Easy Boss," and Pennsylvania's Matt Quay. He thought the conversations went well. Kohlsaat later wrote that Hanna reported to McKinley:

"You can get both New York and Pennsylvania, Governor, but there are certain conditions."

"What are they?"

"They want a promise that you will appoint Tom Platt Secretary of the Treasury, and they want it in writing."

The thick smoke from McKinley's cigar curled to the ceiling of the little den in Lake View, Hanna's Cleveland home. He paced the room. No, the Governor finally replied, the price was too high. Hanna reminded him that this would clinch the nomination.

"I can't do it, Mark."

"Well," sighed Hanna, "we have got to work harder. . . ."

By losing New York and Pennsylvania Hanna soon realized he was gaining something infinitely more important: an always effective campaign slogan—"The People against the Bosses." The strategy of the "bosses" now was to block McKinley with a chain of interlocking regional candidates and favorite sons. Thomas B. Reed of Maine, who had once defeated McKinley for the speakership of the House of Representatives, would hold New England; Platt's candidate would be Levi P. Morton, Harrison's Vice President, whom he called "the safest governor New York ever had"; Quay would present himself as the favorite son of Pennsylvania; former President Harrison would represent Indiana; in the Middle West there were Cullom of Illinois, Davis of Minnesota, Manderson of Nebraska, and Iowa's Allison.

First casualty of the so-called "combine" was Harrison, who preferred to marry his late wife's niece over the objections of his children. This raised the public eyebrow and left the anti-McKinley forces with a motley collection of overripe candidates. At the age of sixty-six, Senator Shelby M. Cullom of Illinois had little to recommend him but a supposed physical likeness to Lincoln; the Chicago *Tribune* dubbed him "the tall, quaking ash of the Sangamon." His senatorial colleague, the suave William Boyd Allison of Iowa, was almost a year older, and the Wall Street banker Morton was even more ancient. According to *Puck,* the Democratic humor magazine, "Morton of New York is willing to become great in a nice, respectable way, providing none of the work is put on his own shoulders. He is 72 years old and at that age one can't work very hard, even at being great. So Mr. Platt takes charge of the details."

By far the most cynical candidacy was that of Senator Quay, the Pennsylvania boss who gorged himself on state funds while quoting Latin and Greek. He blandly announced that he would run on a platform of "municipal reform." The editor of the Philadelphia *Press* confessed that this bit of effrontery had taken his breath away.

Only "Czar" Tom Reed, the brilliant, acerbic Speaker of the House, was more than a cardboard candidate, but to a friend who sought to encourage his bid Reed replied, "The convention could do worse, and probably will." If Reed's inflexibility wasn't to defeat him, his sense of humor would. He stood foursquare for the gold standard; McKinley was keeping quiet on monetary policy, although his record teetered on the edge of free silver, which prompted the Speaker to say, "McKinley does not want to be called a goldbug or a silverbug, so he has compromised on a straddlebug." The more hopeless Reed's chances grew, the wittier he became.

Although Reed's prospects were slim, he still had to

be taken seriously as long as New England backed him. But on March 31, 1896, the New Hampshire Republican convention adopted a platform endorsing both "New England's noble and illustrious son, the Hon. Thomas B. Reed of Maine, and the pure and able statesman and champion of protection, the Hon. William McKinley of Ohio." The leader of the Reed forces, Senator William Chandler, angrily charged that Hanna was running "a boodle canvass" and a "fat-frying" operation. Hanna replied, "Sewer gas must have an outlet, and as for Senator Chandler . . . well, he is simply talking through his hat again." Actually Chandler's blast hurt Reed, for the Senator was himself well known as a less than scrupulous politician. A cartoon in the Washington *Post* was captioned, with more than a dash of irony, "The truly good Mr. Chandler bitterly bewaileth the wicked ways of politics." The mortal blow came a month later when another neighboring state turned its back on Reed and resolved that "in the great apostle of protection, William McKinley of Ohio, we recognize the first choice of the Republicans of Vermont for their personal candidate." Quipped *Judge*, the Republican answer to *Puck*, "Brother Reed was seen to go out with a lighted lantern the other night, and was heard to inquire in a hoarse whisper, 'Seen anything of my boom lately?' "

GEORGE B. LUKS IN *The Verdict*, MARCH 13, 1889

HENRY CLAY

Hanna was deeply hurt by such opposition cartoons as this, which showed him as a cruel, bloated capitalist.

The New York *Journal* poll on April 2 awarded McKinley 413 of the 453½ votes needed for nomination. Only the outcome in Illinois now stood between Hanna's man and victory. Wrote Allison's manager, freely mixing his metaphors, "We must gather up our loins there, for that is the heart of it all." To bring this most crucial state delegation into McKinley's camp Hanna gambled on Charles G. Dawes, who would not turn thirty-one until August 27, 1896, and had never voted in Illinois. After his first meeting with Dawes, early in 1895, Hanna had said to Kohlsaat, "He doesn't *look* [like] much, does he?" Tall, skinny Dawes had grown up in a household in which McKinley was a revered name: his father had been a

Republican congressman from Ohio. Besides devotion to the cause, what may have most recommended him to Hanna was a willingness to work for nothing and to pay his own expenses. This Dawes could well afford: he was already a minor utility magnate with interests in three states. In Illinois within a year and a half the young amateur would weld a group of novices and has-beens into a political organization that would beat Senator Cullom, the favorite son. By April 30 Dawes was able to assert that forty-six of the state's forty-eight convention delegates were committed to McKinley.

The Republican National Convention, which opened in St. Louis on June 16, was an anticlimax. Joe Manley, Reed's manager, had already formally capitulated. Platt and Quay were still putting up window-dressing resistance, but as New York *Tribune* publisher Whitelaw Reid wrote McKinley, since they "must either fall in with the procession or get run over by it, you do not seem to be called upon to offer them many premiums to reward them for not committing suicide."

While waiting for the inevitable, the delegates enjoyed flag-decked St. Louis, whose population of about 610,000 ranked it as the nation's fourth largest city. Young William Allen White, reporting for the Kansas City *World*, arrived in his new five-dollar suit and promptly went off to see *The Bohemian Girl* at an outdoor beer garden. Others who liked their drink harder could sample "The McKinley," a concoction of bourbon, lemon juice, and sugar.

Inside the convention hall, built of ersatz marble at a cost of $75,000, the only fireworks came when weeping Senator Henry Teller of Colorado led a modest walkout of delegates from the silver-mining states in protest over a platform plank that endorsed the "existing gold standard." Reporter White paid a dollar to a North Carolina delegate for a seat directly in front of Mark Hanna and was thus in position to tell his readers that McKinley's manager was the first to shout "Good-bye!" at the departing silverites. If Hanna was feeling crabby it was partly because the intense Missouri heat made him break out in hives, especially around the ankles. Another spectator found the silver walkout of particular interest: William Jennings Bryan, covering the convention for the Omaha *World-Herald,* stood on his desk in the press section to get a better view.

Long-distance telephone wires had been strung to St. Louis, the first such telephonic communication that far west, and in his home on North Market Street in Canton, Ohio, William McKinley pressed to his ear a receiver that curved like the neck of a swan and listened to the roar of delegates shouting his name. The Major was sitting in a heavy armchair taking notes. "Alabama," called the convention clerk. McKinley put down eighteen Alabama votes for McKinley. "Arkansas." When the roll call reached "Ohio," McKinley was over the top.

McKinley had selected a vice-presidential candidate even before the convention opened. He would be Garret Augustus Hobart of New Jersey, longtime state chairman and national committeeman, president or director of water companies, gas companies, manufacturing companies, and railroads. Commented the *Nation,* disapprovingly: "... there were probably not a dozen men in the convention, outside of the New Jersey delegation, who knew anything about his public or business career." William McKinley's nomination cost Marcus Alonzo Hanna $100,000 from his own pocket; the candidate's cousin, Will Osborne of Boston, raised $25,000, and Philander C. Knox gathered another $6,000 from his Pittsburgh friends. Of this achievement *Life* Magazine wrote:

When the Prince of Wales won the Derby the other day with Persimmon he led his horse off to the unsaddling enclosure amid a stupendous expression of the enthusiasm of the spectators. It would have been a great sight to see Mr. Hanna lead Major McKinley off to be weighed after the vote of Ohio was cast at St. Louis, but unfortunately they don't do it in that way at political conventions.

The Republicans did the next best thing. Immediately after the nomination the delegates began

In person, Hanna was pleasant-looking if not handsome, and, for his times, a farsighted businessman.

chanting, "Hanna!" "We want Hanna!" "Speech!" He walked to the platform. The galleries rose to see him better. The delegates rose in tribute. Not long ago the smart politicians had been openly contemptuous. Hanna was a mere businessman. Inexperienced. Presumptuous. Hadn't he opened his campaign a year and a half before the convention? Unheard of! He was leaving his candidate too exposed. Naïve. He was giving his opponents too much time to unite. Inept. But now he stood upon the crest, his hands behind his back, sweat pouring from his fleshy face, acknowledging their cheers. He spoke in a high, thin voice, for he was nervous and he hated public speaking: "What feeble efforts I have contributed to the result, I am here to lay the fruits of it at the feet of my party and upon the altar of my country. [*Applause.*] I am now ready to take my position in the ranks ... and do the duty of a soldier until next November. [*Great applause.*]"

The next morning Good Soldier Hanna was promoted to General as the Republican National Committee unanimously voted him its chairman. It was, the Boston *Evening Transcript* said, the beginning of what would be a new "Hannaverian dynasty."

What manner of man was this Mark Hanna, the king-maker? Physically, he was of average height, five feet nine or ten, with broad shoulders, barrel chest, and slim legs; his skin was like "ruddy terra-cotta"; atop the square head was light hair, faded auburn, now thinning; he had great jug ears and a heavy jaw; his eyes were brown, and when he was provoked they sparkled; he was clean-shaven, but wore long sideburns in the muttonchop style; on his chin was a trace of a dimple. It was a face that failed to hide the emotions behind it, that could wear, a contemporary said, "a smile that covers both hemispheres."

He was a simple man, a plain man; less than an indifferent dresser, he wore cheap suits badly; at the table his preference was for corned-beef hash, made from a Duluth mining-camp recipe, or creamed chipped beef; stewed corn, lima beans, or their conglomerate, succo-

CONTINUED ON PAGE 130

Lights and SHADOWS

History, even the subtlest writing of the most masterful historians, records very imperfectly the homely appearance and flavor of an era, its ordinary pleasures and sorrows, and the special style by which we remember a generation. How did the poor actually look, and how the prosperous? What was the look, for example, of a poor share-cropper family dressed up for church in 1895, or of a street urchin on a sweltering summer day in the slums? How did a jaunty blade of that bygone time tilt his cap, and how did a sober Boston patrician set his feet at a meeting of the board? For answers to questions like these one must turn to the camera, which George Eastman was putting into the hands of ordinary people just as the Nineties began. But picture-taking was still an event, not an everyday affair, and individuals tended to stand like statues; when in a group, they arranged themselves into frozen, carefully planned tableaux. The photographs here and on the next twenty pages are rare, and they are all contemporary. The selection may be arbitrary, but we show them large, to capture as best we can a time now —but for the elderly among us—forever gone.

Leaning coolly on outsize two-wheelers, three Floridians could justly consider themselves modish members of the sporting set. Cycling, which was not introduced here until 1876, enjoyed a great vogue in the 90's. Right: Two young ladies rest in a timeless, demure pose in a wood near the gorge of ever-popular Niagara Falls.

The frontier was closed in 1890, at any rate by historians. Yet Americans reading the news from South Dakota at the end of December, 1890, might well have thought otherwise. So did the Brulé branch of the Sioux nation, whose tepees are seen here. On December 29, 1890, the U.S. Cavalry slaughtered Sioux Indians in the Battle of Wounded Knee Creek, thereby giving the tribe a shattering demonstration that their magical "ghost shirts" would not repel bullets. Alone among the Sioux, the Brulés refused to recognize defeat. They formed a great encampment not far from the Pine Ridge Agency, prepared to hold out till the unknowable end. While their chiefs wrangled in daily conferences and U.S. troops kept vigil on the cold windswept plain, the Brulés, inspired by their Ghost Dance religion, awaited a sign that their moment of deliverance would come. No sign ever came, and even the intransigent Brulés bowed to the inevitable. Their encampment was photographed by J. H. C. Grabill, who was on hand with the watchful Army detachment. It was America's last great gathering of hostile Indians, and it had disbanded by spring.

39

In the shadow of a commodious Staten Island house, some 1,800 miles from Wounded Knee Creek, dozens of Oriental vases and a few pagoda-shaped ornaments fashionably decorate a broad, rolling lawn. The Dutch-style house, almost two hundred years old by 1900, overlooked the Narrows, the entranceway to New York Harbor, and belonged to Alice Austen, member of a prominent New York family. Miss Austen, who was born on Staten Island in 1866, was a tennis and photography enthusiast (she took this picture) during the 1890's; she was also fond of Oriental art objects, a taste then all the rage. One room of the Austen house was covered from floor to ceiling with Oriental fans. Miss Austen, whose neighbors included Vanderbilts, Roosevelts, and Cunards, lost her money and eventually her house after the Wall Street crash of 1929.

41

Not far from rural Staten Island an overworked dray horse, victim of a New York City heat wave, lies dead on a slum street, while children, totally unconcerned about its presence, cool off in an open gutter. In the 1890's, the horse, hauler of wagons, carriages, and many streetcars,

still dominated the urban scene, but he did not make it bucolic. Even then, New Yorkers complained of the noise, filth, and clatter—and the danger to life and limb—from hard-driving wagoners. As for the horses, they were ill-suited to the city and died at a fearful rate in hot weather.

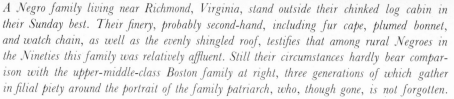

A Negro family living near Richmond, Virginia, stand outside their chinked log cabin in their Sunday best. Their finery, probably second-hand, including fur cape, plumed bonnet, and watch chain, as well as the evenly shingled roof, testifies that among rural Negroes in the Nineties this family was relatively affluent. Still their circumstances hardly bear comparison with the upper-middle-class Boston family at right, three generations of which gather in filial piety around the portrait of the family patriarch, who, though gone, is not forgotten.

Arrayed on and around an enormous horse-drawn coach, a group of Chicago socialites (we do not know their names) prepare to embark en masse on a gay jaunt into the countryside. Coach travel, a grim and jarring necessity before the coming

of the railroad, was revived nostalgically in England and America during the 1890's as a socially impeccable sport. Scorning mere fidelity to old-time coaching, enthusiasts preferred specially built, outsized vehicles like this one, known as "tallyhos."

The "working girl" was one of the much-discussed phenomena of the 1890's. Here are working women of Lynn, Massachusetts, looking for all the world like participants in a church social, as they file out of a shoe factory in 1895. In Lynn, a shoe-manufacturing center from colonial times, almost half the work force consisted of women. Because shoemaking demanded skill, and since machines did the rough work, employment in a shoe factory was deemed, at least in Lynn, a most respectable occupation. The workday of the period was some ten to twelve hours. Women in the factories earned about six dollars a week. (Men doing similar work were paid almost twice as much.) Elsewhere the working girl was often a tougher breed. In New York in 1896, for example, laundresses in the garment industry held a sit-down strike in bold support of their sisters behind the sewing machines. Women also played a prominent part in a mass strike meeting at Cooper Union. A more affluent counterpart of the militant working girl was the equally militant "new woman" of the Nineties. At the big midwestern colleges she began to participate in competitive sports. Forming fervent little cultural clubs, she and her sisters demanded equal rights for their sex. Still, the vast majority of women looked down on both factory work and voting. Men still firmly ruled the country.

48

Looking patrician and sensible in high shoes and creaseless trousers, the board of directors of the Boston Public Library meets in 1894 to discuss, among other things, which new books were fit to purchase and the new library building just designed by the architectural firm of McKim, Mead & White. The trustees include, left to right, Henry W. Haynes,

lawyer, archaeologist, and professor of classics; Frederick Prince, former mayor of Boston; board chairman Samuel A. B. Abbott, lawyer, librarian, and driving force behind the institution for most of his life; the Reverend William R. Richards, a prominent Boston minister; and Phineas Pierce, a leading Boston financier and the board's fiscal expert.

Despite the imaginative ideas of the photographer, sawing logs and splitting timber formed no part of the professional activities of these flouncily clad women in Dawson City, Yukon Territory. They were among the fair (well a little) but frail (unques-

tionably) who had hastened to the boom town after the Klondike gold strike of 1896. Bearing such sobriquets as "Big Sal" and "Golden Gut Flossie," these prostitutes plied their trade in the shanties of Paradise Alley that stand behind them.

In a turn-of-the-century wedding ceremony in rural Sherman County, Oregon, bride and bridegroom stand soberly under a typical paper decoration of the period. The prosperous wheat-growing county had been settled by homesteaders in 1882.

Under a similar paper bower, another Sherman County couple prepare to celebrate their golden wedding anniversary, amid signs of modest rural prosperity including fancy wallpaper, a new stove, and other then-esteemed articles of decor.

Rustic scholars play outside their little frame schoolhouse in rural Maine. During the Nineties many schools through-out the country were introducing manual training, drawing, science, and other new notions into an increasingly complex

curriculum, but the schoolmarm in the old one-room schoolhouse, with her high-necked blouse and her hair in a bun, contin-
ued to do what she had always done: dispense the three R's via old Webster Spellers and McGuffey's unchanging Readers. 57

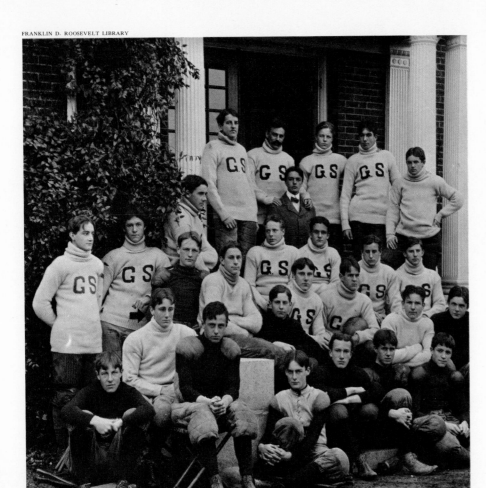

A "most satisfactory" Groton boy and an aspiring football player, he poses with his teammates in 1899.

A student poor in history and languages, he sits with class at Aarau cantonal school, Switzerland, 1896.

58

A Few Time Bombs,

All schools look innocent enough. Yet in every decade some of them will hide under their roofs the great makers and destroyers of the generation to follow. These troublesome figures are disguised as schoolboys, an almost impenetrable form of concealment. Shown here are some of the most noteworthy—and best disguised—boys and young men of the 1890's. At left (arrow) is Franklin Roosevelt at 17, the future architect of the welfare state—the uncertain shape of American democracy in the industrial age. At bottom left (arrow) is Albert Einstein, also at 17, nine years before he revolutionized physics with his special theory of relativity. Immediately below is Vladimir Ilyich Ulyanov, alias "Lenin," in 1892 at the start of his career as the archrevolutionary of world Communism. Below Lenin is the Scotsman Alexander

A 22-year-old Russian lawyer and son of a faithful public servant

An Italian seminarian, 20 years old in 1901, soon to be ordained

A London shipping clerk in 1900, later excelled in medicine

Waiting to Explode

Fleming, about 28 years before he discovered penicillin and helped usher in the population explosion. Left of Fleming is Angelo Roncalli, who would be known 57 years later as Pope John XXIII, Catholicism's great modernizing spirit. At right above is Adolf Hitler (arrow) at ten, the twentieth century's contribution to history's select list of supremely evil men. Below right is Henry Ford (arrow), who invented the assembly line and multiplied many times the might of modern industry. Directly below, as a little blond child, is General Charles de Gaulle, leader and symbol of France. To his left is Mohandas K. Gandhi, apostle of nonviolent resistance, nemesis of empire. At bottom is Pablo Picasso, the originally quite traditional painter whose long life epitomizes the revolution of twentieth-century art.

"A little ringleader" by self-description, he sits with his primary-school class near Linz, Austria, 1899.

Edison Company's crack mechanic, with colleagues in Detroit, 1893: he is at work on a new engine.

RADIO TIMES HULTON PICTURE LIBRARY

COLLECTION VIOLLET

A bright young lawyer in 1897, practicing among Indians in Natal in South Africa

The long-haired son of a French philosophy professor, born in 1890

KINDLER VERLAG, MUNICH

The 15-year-old son of a Spanish drawing master, shown in 1896

FORD ARCHIVES, HENRY FORD MUSEUM, DEARBORN, MICHIGAN

MORGAN to the RESCUE

As the nation's gold reserves drained away, panic loomed. Even the President was helpless; he had to turn to someone more powerful

By ANDY LOGAN

J. Pierpont Morgan

At three o'clock in the morning on February 5, 1895, a tall, stout man with white hair, fierce gray eyes, and a monstrous red nose sat playing solitaire in his suite at the Arlington Hotel in Washington, D.C. He had been playing for hours, vigorously forcing the cards into sequence on the table in front of him as if the opportunity to impose order on any situation, even on pieces of cardboard, gave him special satisfaction on this dark morning. The only sounds in the room were the slap of the cards and the occasional striking of a match as he lit still another long black cigar. The sound he was listening for was the peal of the telephone on the wall beside him. Diagonally across Lafayette Square the White House lights were also burning in Grover Cleveland's second-floor office, as they had burned every night for the past two weeks. The solitaire player was J. Pierpont Morgan, and the call he was waiting for was from the Attorney General to say that the President would see him later that morning in time to permit him to save the nation from bankruptcy.

Although Morgan regarded all politicians as incompetents and Democratic officeholders as a lower form of life, he and the Democratic President had much in common. They were almost identical in age, having been born in the same spring of 1837, and were similarly strong-willed, obstinate, blunt-spoken, and, though massively built and homely, attractive to women. Morgan represented the third generation of family wealth, while Cleveland had run for office as a man of the people, come up the hard way; but, affluence aside, their forebears had included about the same percentage of firebrand Puritans, early Harvard and Yale graduates, Protestant dignitaries, civic leaders, and eccentrics. The most significant attribute the two men shared in the winter of 1895, however, was their philosophy of money: they were both devout gold men.

A long and complex series of events had brought the two most powerful men in America to their separate vigils on either side of Lafayette Square. The country's most bitter and divisive quarrel since Appomattox was over money, and the opposing battle colors were gold and silver. By 1895 many of the men who favored the cause of silver sincerely believed that all conflicts between the naturally hostile forces of civilization—capital against labor, conservative against radical, creditor against debtor, soulless corporation against individual, rich businessman against poor farmer—would be resolved in favor of the have-nots if only they could overthrow the *de facto* gold standard which then prevailed in the United States.

To the silverites this partiality for gold was the work of a sinister conspiracy of Wall Street "goldbugs," as they called the enemy forces. (In one of its ruder moments the Atlanta *Constitution* had called Wall Street "a hotbed of goldbuggery.") The fact was that when Congress had passed a law in 1875 making the nation's then-depreciated "greenback" paper money redeemable in "coin" after 1879—that is, in either silver or gold, the ratio then being sixteen ounces of silver to one of gold—silver had been scarce and precious. It had been the opening up of vast silver mines in the West during the following decade and the abandonment of a silver standard by most major nations that had caused the lighter metal to decline drastically in value. In the Nineties the silver in a silver dollar was worth less than forty-nine cents in gold, and businessmen redeeming greenbacks (that is, as opposed to silver or gold certificates) at the Treasury had no problem deciding which coin to specify. Moreover, the law required the government to reissue such bills, and thus the same piece of paper could be redeemed in gold again and again. Gold is heavy in the pocket for ordinary business transactions, however, and the pace of the gold drain stayed well short of a run so long as times were moderately prosperous and people had confidence that their greenbacks were good as gold at the Treasury window.

For bankers, businessmen, and much of the general public the signal for the ending of that confidence was the sinking of the government gold reserve below a hundred million dollars. When it had begun redeeming greenbacks in coin in 1879, the Treasury had set that amount of gold as the minimum to be kept on hand for redemption purposes. The sum had no intrinsic or legal force (there were over three and a half times that many greenbacks out, for example), but over the years it had taken on what Cleveland later described as "a superstitious sanctity," which had millions of Americans convinced that with $101,000,000 in gold reserves the monetary system was sound, while a drop to $99,000,000 threatened dire calamity. The calamitous hour had arrived in the spring of 1893, shortly after Cleveland's second inauguration. For the next four years much of his energies were given over to finding gold to pump into the dwindling reserve and watching it drain away as fast as he supplied it.

The silverites viewed this frustrating struggle without even crocodile tears. "They can't exhaust the gold reserve too quickly to suit me," declared a pro-silver congressman from Missouri. For a decade they had been clamoring for unlimited (or free) silver coinage at the old, unrealistic ratio of sixteen to one, although, despite vigorous administration efforts to force it into circulation, nearly $700,000,000 worth of unwanted silver already lay idle in the Treasury vaults. Government purchases of silver had now been halted, but if there were no more gold in the Treasury, the country would be perforce on a silver standard, a situation equivalent to a fifty per cent devaluation. The argument that the money of all the major nations was based on gold and that

ninety per cent of U.S. foreign trade was with this gold bloc carried no weight with the silverites. "What have we got to do with abroad?" demanded one of them on the floor of the Senate.

Before 1893 the silverites had been a comparatively minor, aberrant sect, almost equally troublesome to both major parties. Although their strength, like that of the Democrats, lay in the West and South, Cleveland, a gold man, had been easily elected in 1892. By the middle of his term, however, he had become more and more isolated politically. With the conversion to silverism of that great commoner from the West, William Jennings Bryan, the silverites, joined by the Populists, had begun to rally other Democrats to their cause. Their simplistic crusade grew in strength because it offered hope, however irrational, to millions of desperate Americans who saw no hope elsewhere. During the mid-Nineties the country was in the savage grip of a depression that followed the

BY F. VICTOR GILLAM IN *Judge*, March 7, 1896

WILL IT RISE?

This anti-Cleveland cartoon shows the President, who has lost his halo, anxiously stoking the gold-reserve thermometer with government bonds. With public bond issues—and Morgan's indispensable aid—the country weathered the storm. But the Democratic party did less well.

Panic of 1893. Over five hundred banks and loan companies had failed, hurting the small depositor hardest. There was a glut of agricultural products on the world market, and the farmers were being crushed between ten cent corn and ten per cent mortgages. A large share of the mortgages were payable to banks in Wall Street which, in the silverites' code, had fomented the '93 panic in the first place. Thus the traditional mistrust of the agrarian West and South for the urban Northeast—"the enemy's country," Bryan called it—was concentrated on that narrow Manhattan canyon. To the debtors of the nation, reported *Harper's Weekly* in 1894, Wall Street was "a dark, mysterious, crafty, wicked, rapacious and tyrannical power," and only the inflationary effect of free silver could liberate them from this enfeoffment to the goldbugs.

With the talk of a silver standard, banking and commercial institutions inevitably took fright and began to pay all customs and internal revenue debts in silver, at the same time exchanging their greenbacks at the Treasury for gold, which they either hoarded or shipped abroad. The reserve, which Cleveland had precariously maintained just below the hundred million mark during most of 1893, fell to sixty-five million early the next year, and the specter of default and devaluation had now moved out of the realm of superstition. The stricken South and West were in no position to come to Cleveland's rescue, even if they had been so minded, and he turned to Wall Street for help.

Much of the subsequent liaison between the Street and the Treasury was handled by August Belmont. Belmont was both a goldbug and a leading citizen of the enemy's country, having five years earlier succeeded his father as head of August Belmont and Company, the American representatives of the Rothschilds. He was also that rarity among international bankers, a Democrat. Several times a month during the recurrent gold crises of 1894 someone from the Treasury would come up from Washington and go directly to Belmont's office for a briefing on ways and means. Once or twice it was the Secretary himself, the white-haired Kentuckian and former Speaker of the House, John G. Carlisle. Carlisle, however, was a frontier figure who had spent his early political years baiting Wall Street and, although he was now foursquare for gold, he was never at ease with rich easterners. The Treasury delegate was usually Assistant Secretary William Edmund Curtis, a handsome, earnest young lawyer from an old New York family who had first encountered Belmont at the Racquet Club. Because of the political perils of trafficking with Wall Street, and the danger that public knowledge of such pilgrimages would make the Treasury situation seem even grimmer than it was and thus set off a further gold drain, Curtis' visits to Belmont were usually clandestine affairs. He would then move on to secret interviews with other Wall Street leaders, who would greet him much as if they were plenipotentiaries of a wealthy foreign state granting an audience to an emissary from a poor and politically misguided nation. "It might have been imagined that it was Turkey or China which was standing, hat in hand, in the money market," wrote an economist of the time.

Twice during 1894 the Treasury had succeeded in bolstering the reserve through the public sale of a fifty-million-dollar bond issue. Though paid for in gold, these were coin bonds—that is, principal and interest were to be paid off in either gold or silver. The silver-minded Congress declined to authorize more marketable bonds specifically payable in gold, although the saving in interest would have been substantial. The small investor rejected both 1894 bond issues, and it was as a result of Curtis' and Belmont's maneuvers that they were taken up by a group of New York banks in the first instance and, in the second, by a syndicate that included the man who would be found playing solitaire at the Arlington Hotel that early morning in February, 1895. Morgan had been widely commended for his public spirit in financial circles the year before. James Stillman, of the National City Bank, later claimed that it had been he who had raised much of the second 1894 fund after a desperate appeal from Morgan, but that Morgan "became perfectly bombastic and triumphant as the savior of his country." Stillman complained: "He took all the credit. But then, you see, he is a poet! Morgan is a poet!"

The 1894 bond issues had provided only ephemeral relief, since it developed that many of the purchasers had merely bought them with gold withdrawn from the Treasury reserve the bond issues were meant to replenish. As the threat of gold default grew stronger, the rate of withdrawal naturally picked up speed. During the month of January, 1895, the drain amounted to forty-five million dollars, with over twenty-five million of this going abroad. The western senator who had told Congress a few weeks before that "when there's a run on the United States Treasury, there'll be a run on the Maker of the Universe," was now publicly silent, perhaps privately saying his prayers. On January 28 Cleveland sent a message to Congress requesting congressional action, which was not forthcoming, and declaring that if the country were forced onto a silver standard, it would become a second-class nation.

On the evening of Thursday, January 30, when Curtis arrived in New York in the midst of this worst gold crisis of them all, a secret conference with Belmont was no longer easy to arrange. Withdrawals from the gold reserve that day had come to $3,750,000, and it was down to less than $42,000,000, or, at this rate of loss, about eleven days' supply. The situation, trumpeted the *New York Times*, "involves the honor of the United States throughout the world." New York newspapermen, knowing that Washington would have to take some action, had been meeting trains all day. When Curtis stepped out that evening on the platform at Jersey City, then the nearest terminal of the Pennsylvania Railroad, a dozen reporters were waiting for him. They followed him on the Cortlandt Street ferry but were turned away at the door of Belmont's town house, where the two men had agreed to meet. In the upstairs library Belmont and Curtis now reviewed the situation. For political reasons Cleveland and Carlisle favored trying to obtain gold through still another public sale of bonds, hoping they would not have to turn again to Wall Street. But even if the general public were to buy the coin bonds it had twice rejected the year before, the rate of the gold drain was now so precipitate that the reserve would vanish before the ritual of public bidding could be completed. The week before, Belmont had been so distressed by the situation that he had gone down to Washington on his own to talk to Carlisle. The only remedy for the Treasury's current predicament, he had reminded the Secretary, was an enormous influx of gold from abroad, which would then bring the gold out of hiding in this country. Only an international syndicate could bring about such a reversal, he had pointed out. Without committing himself, Carlisle had asked Belmont to inquire of the Rothschilds in London whether they would be able to find European buyers for U.S. coin bonds. Now Belmont handed Curtis a sheaf of cables from the Rothschilds saying it could not be done. For several moments Belmont and Curtis sat in gloomy silence. "You'll have to see Morgan," Belmont said finally. "He's the only man who can help now."

Before he went to bed that night at the University Club, Curtis sent off a letter to Carlisle describing the city as "nervous and panicky." Soon after breakfast the next morning he appeared on the doorstep of Morgan's brownstone mansion in East Thirty-sixth Street. In spite of the growing alarm in the financial world, the head of the Wall Street power structure had not made any move. Apparently he had been standing on ceremony, waiting to be asked. Now he agreed to meet with Curtis and Belmont at the Subtreasury building that afternoon. A few minutes later he cabled his London partners, who in a return cable explained that they had already been consulted on the situation by the Rothschilds and that, in view of the emergency, they were willing to work with the Rothschilds on the European sale of a bond issue if Morgan would work with Belmont in New York. But they endorsed the Rothschild verdict that Europe would not buy American bonds that were not specifically payable in gold.

Belmont met Morgan at his office at 23 Wall Street shortly after noon, and when the two bankers crossed the street to the Subtreasury, it was observed that the dapper, mustachioed Belmont was walking a little to the rear. He was, after all, sixteen years younger than the fifty-eight-year-old Morgan, who had been used to doing business with the elder Belmont. Thereafter "Augie" Belmont accepted gracefully his relegation to the role of junior partner in the enterprise. During the three-hour conference that followed, Morgan agreed to take over direction of the rescue mission, but only if he would be in full charge. Dubious as the prospects seemed, he went on, "I will undertake to get the gold necessary abroad, *provided it is left in my hands to undertake. . . .*" He wrote out a memorandum of his plan of action for Curtis, who got ready to leave for Washington with it.

By mid-afternoon the bare information that Morgan and Belmont were inside the Subtreasury had already checked the run on the reserve. The Treasury's loss for the day was nearly a million and a half dollars less than that of the day before. A throng of reporters and Wall Street figures, seeking reassurance, surrounded the two bankers as they left the building. They refused to answer any questions, but Curtis, emerging a few minutes later, gave the crowd an answer of sorts: he was smiling broadly. That night the banking firm of Lazard Frères brought back to the Treasury four million dollars in gold that it had already packed for shipment abroad.

The detailed cable that Morgan sent off to his London partners after he returned to 23 Wall Street that afternoon did not unnerve them by describing the new undertaking in terms of their duty as self-sacrificing philanthropists. To "avert calamity," read the cable, he proposed that the government make a private contract with a pair of syndicates—one of them managed by the Morgan and Belmont companies in New York and the other by the Morgan firm working with the Rothschilds in London—which would agree to provide the Treasury with gold to the extent of at least fifty million dollars, the gold to be paid for with a new coin bond issue, which the syndicates would then auction off themselves. Blandly ignoring his colleagues' judgment that coin bonds could

Banker August Belmont, liaison between Washington and Wall Street

CONTINUED ON PAGE 138

63

In the Nineties the American garden of art
blossomed with a bouquet of European cuttings—impressionism,
Pre-Raphaelitism, realism. But the public
looked upon the gorgeous display with a suspicious eye
and sniffed with a critical nose, for it was a time

When Everyone Knew What He Liked

By DAVID G. LOWE

*One of the prime evidences of affluence in the last decade of
the nineteenth century was a room overstuffed with paintings. The gallery in Mrs. Potter Palmer's Chicago mansion
(above) was a supreme example of this kind of ostentation.*

When in 1872 William Merritt Chase was asked if he would like to go abroad, the young painter, living in St. Louis, replied, "My God, I'd rather go to Europe than go to heaven." He did go—to Munich for five years—and returned to teach in New York and become one of the most influential painters in America.

Chase's attitude toward Europe typifies a sentiment common among Americans in the last quarter of the nineteenth century, a sentiment that captured writers like Henry James, architects like Stanford White, lady art collectors like Isabella Stewart Gardner, financiers like J. P. Morgan, and scholars like Bernard Berenson. By the Nineties, what had been a sentiment had become a passion. While it is true that Americans had been going to Europe since the days of Benjamin Franklin and John Singleton Copley, the increasing wealth of the United States and the advent of steamships and railroads made it incomparably easier and faster to get there.

But there was another, a more important factor in this Nineties rush to Europe. The old, unified Anglo-Saxon American culture, symbolized by a white Congregational church on a New England village green, was cracking apart. That America, reflected in the landscapes of Frederick Church and in the conversation pieces of Eastman Johnson, was disappearing. And going with it was the earlier nationalistic self-confidence that America was a land possessed of all the answers, that all the sophistication one needed could be obtained in a hut in a wood by a pond. Many things had contributed to this change: the shocking carnage of the Civil War, the increasing immigration from Europe—especially of the well-educated Germans—the industrialization that was gathering millions into cities. Growing rich and big but unsure, the republic suddenly turned outward, to Europe, for instruction.

No group was more directly affected by this reversal than were the painters of America. If Chase wanted to go to Europe, so did Frank Duveneck of Covington, Kentucky; Childe Hassam of Dorchester, Massachusetts; Thomas Eakins of Philadelphia; and Abbott Thayer of Boston. And they all went: Duveneck, like Chase, to Munich; Hassam, Thayer, and Eakins to Paris. In fact, there was not a significant American painter of the decade who did not go abroad, and most went for prolonged study. The visitors studied with painters like Wilhelm Leibl, Jean Léon Gérôme, and Claude Monet, and when they returned they were technically the best-trained generation in the history of American art.

When they returned they brought in their paint boxes all the new ideas that had broken forever the grip of academic painting on the ateliers of Europe. These changes are revealed in the French impressionism of Hassam, J. Alden Weir, and Chase; in the Munich style of atmospheric realism of Duveneck; in the French objective realism of Eakins and Thomas Anshutz; in the English Pre-Raphaelite echoes of Thomas Dewing and Thayer. They submerged forever the old unity of American painting that had expressed itself in the romanticism of the Hudson River School and in the sentimental genre subjects of artists like George Caleb Bingham. The old schools survived in men like J. G. Brown and E. L. Henry, but compared to the fresh realism of Everett Shinn, they were as dated as "Tenting on the Old Camp Ground" in an evening of the new ragtime.

But if the European fever had infected America's painters, it had also struck the rich men who bought pictures. In the 1850's and 60's artists like Jaspar Cropsey could earn a secure and handsome living from their work, but the advent of the photograph, which replaced the lucrative standard portrait, and the rage for Europe changed all that. While Eakins was having difficulty selling a single one of his superb pictures, A. T. Stewart, the New York dry-goods prince, was paying a reputed $75,000 for a painting by the minor French artist Meissonier, and Mrs. Gardner was offering nearly $200,000 for Gainsborough's *Blue Boy*. Mrs. Potter Palmer's gallery in her $700,000 Chicago castle (opposite) was filled not with native paintings but with works by French impressionists.

It is true that there were always some discerning collectors of American canvases, such as Thomas B. Clarke of New York, the great patron of Winslow Homer, and Charles Lang Freer, the Detroit industrialist who bought the canvases of the expatriate James McNeill Whistler. But these were the exceptions, and most talented painters of the Nineties earned their living in other ways than by selling their oils. Some, like E. H. Blashfield and Thayer, did murals; others, like Everett Shinn and Edwin Austin Abbey, were book and magazine illustrators; but many more—Eakins, Anshutz, Weir—taught painting. Since there were no ready-made public monuments for sale in Europe, American sculptors like Augustus Saint-Gaudens—trained in Paris and Rome—fared better than the painters. One American painter, John Singer Sargent, did have a great success. But he had been born in Italy and had lived so long abroad that it was easy to forget his origins.

At the Columbian Exposition in Chicago in 1893, attention was centered not on American paintings but on the 126 foreign masterpieces owned by Americans. Ironically, the American paintings at Chicago were severely criticized because they reflected European schools and because they did not depict scenes from American history. "Among all this collection of more than 1,000 paintings in oil," the semiofficial *Book of the Fair* pontificated, "there is not one of special excellence, and there are not a dozen in all, which treat of the annals of our country." This of a show that included nine Sargents, Eakins' great *Agnew Clinic,* illustrations by Charles Dana Gibson and Frederic Remington, and Chase's lovely *Alice.*

The passion for Europe had won. Berenson preached an aestheticism that glorified Italy, and Mrs. Gardner built a Venetian palace in Boston and filled it with proper European pictures. The English dealer Joseph Duveen took Morgan by the hand, and the Metropolitan Museum got pictures from every corner of the world but America. Henry Adams wrote that in this period his native land had lost its self-confi-

dence and that "the self-distrust became introspection
—nervous self-consciousness—irritable dislike of America." It was in the Nineties that the Harvard aesthete
Charles Eliot Norton proclaimed that "in America
even the shadows are vulgar." The century closed with
Shinn trying desperately to sell an illustration to
Harper's, with Duveneck teaching in Cincinnati, and
with Eakins in his deepest obscurity. It was a dozen
years before patrons of the stature of Gertrude Vanderbilt Whitney came to the aid of American art.

*Murals were lavishly commissioned for
the Renaissance-style edifices that
sprang up across the country in the
Nineties. Because of the multitude of
muralists—men such as Edwin Blashfield and J. Alden Weir—working on
the Chicago World's Fair, Augustus
Saint-Gaudens exclaimed to a friend:
"Do you realize that this is the greatest
meeting of artists since the fifteenth
century?" Elihu Vedder's* Rome,
*painted for the Bowdoin College art
gallery, is an excellent example of the
work of the decade. Vedder, a New
Yorker who lived in Rome from 1867
until his death in 1923, was deeply
influenced by classical history. This
mural, with its asexual nudes, olive
trees, and winged scribes, proclaims
the highly personal mythology he constructed from the ancient legends.*

67

METROPOLITAN MUSEUM OF ART, GIFT OF GEORGE A. HEARN, 1913

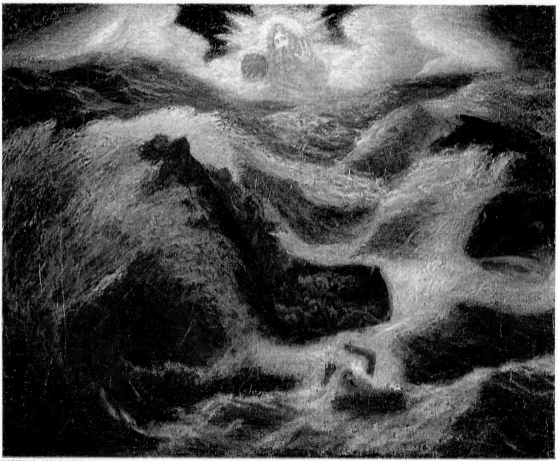

NATIONAL COLLECTION OF FINE ARTS, SMITHSONIAN INSTITUTION

Literature and mythology were rich mines for the artists of the Nineties, as in King Lear's Daughters *(above), by the Philadelphia-born illustrator Edwin Austin Abbey, or* Jonah *(left), by Albert Pinkham Ryder, a painter from New Bedford, Massachusetts, who led a solitary life in New York and whose dark canvases often reflect his love of the sea. Louis Maurer, one of Currier and Ives' stable of painters, composed a still life (below) on the theme of a popular Nineties novel,* Trilby, *by George du Maurier, a tale of a vain but talented artist. To the right is* Diana, *Roman goddess of the hunt, by sculptor Augustus Saint-Gaudens.*

69

Americans in the Nineties dearly loved a sentimental picture, one that would touch the heart and bring a tear to the eye. Fortunately there was a plentiful supply of painters—most of them excellently trained in Europe— who could satisfy this demand. Above right: Edward Lamson Henry's News Office *is typical of the many recreations of eighteenth and early nineteenth century America upon which his popularity rested. See the spooners! See the village gossips! So true to life! Henry, who studied in Paris, had done splendid Civil War sketches, and painted railroads superbly.*

J. G. Brown's The Young Surgeon, *right, is the work of a painter trained at the Academy in Edinburgh; Brown's early painting showed great promise, but his sticky, sentimental portrayals of ragged New York waifs were so much in demand that he spent most of his life endlessly repeating that one tiresome subject.*

One of the favorite personae of the sentimental artist

was the newsboy, sometimes crippled but always appeal-
ing. At left you have him selling a paper in front of the
old New York Herald, in a canvas by N. N. Hyneman.

Breaking Home Ties (above, left), by Thomas Hovenden of Philadelphia, was one of the most famous paintings of the Nineties and the hit of the Chicago World's
Fair. It was admired for its sentimental appeal and also
for its artistic brilliance. This type of life-sized "picture
that told a story" was introduced into America by Hovenden after his study in Paris, where it was very much the
fashion. Hovenden, who came from Ireland, was a superb craftsman who became a beloved teacher at the
Pennsylvania Academy, where Eakins had taught. He
was killed at fifty-four while manfully trying to save a
little girl at a rail crossing. Breaking Home Ties deeply
affected an America in which the young sons of rural
families were succumbing in ever-increasing numbers to
the alluring glitter and rarely found gold of the city.

One of the dominant themes of American art in the Nineties was the idealization of women. When John Singer Sargent painted the Wyndham sisters in all their lush late Victorian elegance (at right) there was no mistaking that these were ladies. At left we have a typical canvas by Thomas Dewing, who specialized in women seated in atmospheric interiors— here, one practices upon her spinet— or wandering through fields of tall grass. This again was Woman as idealized by Man. Carrying matters further, Abbott Thayer was famous for his paintings of females who were in fact virginal angels robed in spotless white, like the little darling at lower left. Then, of course, there was the handsomely dressed lady, and she was caught by J. Alden Weir in her narcissistic pose before a mirror.

A Friendly Call *vibrates with all the virtuosity and sensitivity that its creator, William Merritt*

Chase, acquired in Europe. It is a remarkable piece of social commentary and technical bravura.

The world of men was a topic that had enormous appeal to the realist painters of the Nineties. Between Rounds *(left), by Thomas Eakins, is one of the many pictures that artist did of prize fights. This one, at the arena that stood at Broad and Cherry streets in Philadelphia, is a testament to Eakins' realism, for all the spectators are portraits; the timer is Clarence W. Cranmer, a newspaperman friend of Eakins; and the fighter is one Billy Smith. In the oil above, Thomas Anshutz caught the unlovely grimness of America's new industrial civilization in* Steel Workers' Noontime. *Born in Kentucky of German parentage, Anshutz studied in Paris and went on to teach at the Pennsylvania Academy, where he became one of the great forces behind realism in American painting. Below: The face of the successful businessman of the period is portrayed in this canvas by Edwin Howland Blashfield—better known for his murals in the Library of Congress and the Iowa capitol—of Charles Edwin Wilbour and his two cousins, Isaac Wilbour Brownell and Isaac Champney Wilbour. Charles Wilbour was a writer and a famous Egyptologist.*

77

The city—that booming phenomenon of mansions and hovels, of avenues and junk heaps—into which Americans were thronging was a major subject for the painters of the Nineties. In the picture at left, Childe Hassam has portrayed lower Fifth Avenue in the spring of 1890 with bright impressionist color. The arch is the temporary wooden one designed by Stanford White in 1889 for the centennial of Washington's inauguration. The present stone one was erected six years later. Above: Everett Shinn's picture of Broadway in front of the old Metropolitan Opera clearly displays the beginning of the revolt against the European-oriented aestheticism of painters like Hassam. Though both Shinn and his mentor, the painter Robert Henri, were under the spell of the French impressionists, they wanted American artists to regain their self-confidence, to look at their own country without preconceptions, and then to record honestly what they found.

79

Henry Mills Alden, editor of Harper's, *refused anything that "could not be read aloud in the home."*

Richard Watson Gilder, a poet and the editor of Century, *fought Tammany, tariffs, and tenements.*

Thomas Bailey Aldrich, the Atlantic Monthly *editor from 1881 to 1890, set standards of literary taste.*

Samuel Sidney McClure launched his own erratic, but nonetheless highly popular magazine in 1893.

To be a man of letters in the last decade of the nineteenth century was a great and dignified thing. Something of what that meant can be glimpsed in the four portraits at the left, all of them taken by a notable photographer named George Collins Cox, who specialized in literary personages. Cox was befriended and encouraged by Richard Watson Gilder, the great editor of the Century Magazine.

In the Nineties, as in our own time, literary men and women moved in coteries. Some were geographical, based on the raw new Chicago, on bustling San Francisco, on dwindling Boston, and on the bohemias of New York. Some were based on mutual sympathies —the worlds of reform, of newspapers, of belles-lettres. There was also a bearded Establishment whose work was (in most cases) largely past. James Russell Lowell, Oliver Wendell Holmes, George William Curtis, John Greenleaf Whittier—all these would die in the early part of the decade, to appear no more on ceremonial platforms. William Dean Howells, the dean of belles-lettres, hovered on the edge, encouraging the young realists, but all of them—even Mark Twain, under his real name—rejoiced in three sonorous names, which were recited by readers and lecturegoers almost as a litany.

Walt Whitman (observe, there are only two names, and one foreshortened) was not really in the club, and he died in 1892. And another of the greatest American writers of the century, Herman Melville, dwelt in almost forgotten obscurity. Here is his complete obituary, from the New York Times *of September 29, 1891: "Herman Melville died yesterday at his residence, 104 East Twenty-sixth Street, this city, of heart failure, aged seventy-two. He was the author of* Typee, Omoo, Mobie Dick [*sic*], *and other seafaring tales, written in earlier years. He leaves a wife and two daughters, Mrs. M. B. Thomas and Miss Melville." But if the age missed with Melville, it was a golden one, a watershed between the romantic and realistic in American writing. The gentlemen at left helped preside over it all, and some impression of what they were reading and publishing may be gained from our Nineties Reader.*◆

A Nineties Reader

The View from Abroad

Our selection of work by writers popular in the 1890's commences with a classic. The American Commonwealth, *a broad social and political study of the United States, was written by James Bryce after extensive travels here in the late nineteenth century; later, from 1907 to 1913, he served as ambassador to this country. One wonders if in that post he was not sometimes embarrassed by the chapter entitled "Why Great Men Are Not Chosen Presidents." This is how it begins:*

Europeans often ask, and Americans do not always explain, how it happens that this great office, the greatest in the world, unless we except the Papacy, to which any man can rise by his own merits, is not more frequently filled by great and striking men? . . . But since the heroes of the Revolution died out with Jefferson and Adams and Madison some sixty years ago, no person except General Grant has reached the chair whose name would have been remembered had he not been President, and no President except Abraham Lincoln has displayed rare or striking qualities in the chair. Who now knows or cares to know anything about the personality of James K. Polk . . . ?

Several reasons may be suggested for the fact, which Americans are themselves the first to admit.

One is that the proportion of first-rate ability drawn into politics is smaller in America than in most European countries. . . . In France and Italy, where half-revolutionary conditions have made public life exciting and accessible; in Germany, where an admirably organized civil service cultivates and develops statecraft with unusual success; in England, where many persons of wealth and leisure seek to enter the political arena, while burning questions touch the interests of all classes and make men eager observers of the combatants, the total quantity of talent devoted to parliamentary or administrative work is far larger, relatively to the population, than in America, where much of the best ability, both for thought and for action, for planning and for executing, rushes into a field which is comparatively narrow in Europe, the business of developing the material resources of the country.

Another is that the methods and habits of Congress, and indeed of political life generally, seem to give fewer opportunities for personal distinction, fewer modes in which a man may commend himself to his countrymen by eminent capacity in thought, in speech, or in administration, than is the case in the free countries of Europe.

. . . The ordinary American voter does not object to mediocrity. He has a lower conception of the qualities requisite to make a statesman than those who direct public opinion in Europe have. He likes his candidate to be sensible, vigorous, and, above all, what he calls "magnetic," and does not value, because he sees no need for, originality or profundity, a fine culture or a wide knowledge. Candidates are selected to be run for nomination by knots of persons who, however expert as party tacticians, are usually commonplace men; and the choice between those selected for nomination is made by a very large body, an assembly of over eight hundred delegates from the local party organizations over the country, who are certainly no better than ordinary citizens.

It must also be remembered that the merits of a President are one thing and those of a candidate another thing. An eminent American is reported to have said to friends who wished to put him forward, "Gentlemen, let there be no mistake. I should make a good President, but a very bad candidate." Now to a party it is more important that its nominee should be a good candidate than that he should turn out a good President. A nearer danger is a greater danger. . . . It will be a misfortune to the party, as well as to the country, if the candidate elected should prove a bad President. But it is a greater misfortune to the party that it should be beaten in the impending election, for the evil of losing national patronage will have come four years sooner.

Social distinctions, or the absence of them, equally fascinated Lord Bryce:

There is no rank in America, that is to say, no external and recognized stamp, marking one man as entitled to any social privileges, or to deference and respect from others. No man is entitled to think himself better than his fellows, or to expect any exceptional consideration to be shown by them to him. There is no such thing as a recognized order of precedence, either on public occasions or at a private party, except that yielded to a few official persons, such as the governor and chief judges of a State within that State, as well as to the President and Vice-President, the Speaker of the House, the Federal senators, the judges of the Supreme Federal Court, and the members of the President's cabinet everywhere through the Union. In fact, the idea of a regular "rule of precedence" displeases the Americans. . . . Even men of the highest official rank do not give themselves airs on the score of their position. Some years ago, being in Washington, I was taken by a friend to be presented to the Commander-in-chief of the United States Army, a great soldier whose fame all the world knows. We found him standing at a desk in a bare room in the War Department, at work with one clerk. While he was talking to us the door of the room was pushed open, and there appeared the figure of a Western tourist belonging to what Europeans would call the lower middle class, followed by his wife and sister, who were "doing" Washington. Perceiving that the room was occupied they began to retreat, but the Commander-in-chief called them back. "Walk in, ladies," he said. "You can look around. You won't disturb me; make yourselves at home."

. . . [The] railway kings are among the greatest men, perhaps I may say are the greatest men, in America. They have wealth, else they could not hold the position. They have fame, for every one has heard of their achievements; every newspaper chronicles their movements. They have power, more power—that is, more opportunity of making their personal will prevail —than perhaps any one in political life, except the President and the Speaker, who after all hold theirs only for four years and two years, while the railroad monarch may keep his for life. When the master of one of the greatest Western lines travels towards the Pacific on his palace car, his journey is like a royal progress. Governors of States and Territories bow before him; legislatures receive him in solemn session; cities and towns seek to propitiate him, for has he not the means of making or marring a city's fortunes? Although the railroad companies are unpopular, and although this autocratic sway from a distance contributes to their unpopularity, I do not think that the ruling magnates are themselves generally disliked. On the contrary, they receive that tribute of admiration which the American gladly pays to whoever has done best what every one desires to do.

Lord Bryce also cast his eye upon that perennially fascinating phenomenon, the American woman:

Custom allows to women a greater measure of freedom in doing what they will and going where they please than they have in any European country, except, perhaps, in Russia. No one is surprised to see a lady travel alone from the Atlantic to the Pacific, nor a girl of the richer class walking alone through the streets of a city. If a lady enters some occupation heretofore usually reserved to men, she is subject to much less censorious remark than would follow her in Europe . . .

In no country are women, and especially young women, so much made of. The world is at their feet. Society seems organized for the purpose of providing enjoyment for them. Parents, uncles, aunts, elderly friends, even brothers, are ready to make their comfort and convenience bend to the girls' wishes. The wife has fewer opportunities for reigning over the world of amusements, because, except among the richest people, she has more to do in household management than in England, owing to the scarcity of servants. But she holds in her own house a more prominent, if not a more substantially powerful, position than in England or even in France. . . .

In the farther West, that is to say, beyond the Mississippi, in the Rocky Mountain and Pacific States, one is much struck by what seems the absence of the humblest class of women. The trains are full of poorly dressed and sometimes (though less frequently) rough-mannered men. One discovers no women whose dress or air marks them out as the wives, daughters, or sisters of these men, and wonders whether the male population is celibate, and if so, why there are so many women. Closer observation shows that the wives, daughters, and sisters are there, only their attire and manner are those of what Europeans would call middle class and not working class people. This is partly due to the fact that Western men affect a rough dress. Still one may say that the remark so often made that the masses of the American people correspond to the middle class of Europe is more true of the women than of the men, and is more true of them in the rural districts and in the West than it is of the inhabitants of Atlantic cities. I remember to have been dawdling in a book store in a small town in Oregon when a lady entered to inquire if a monthly magazine, whose name was unknown to me, had yet arrived. When she was gone I asked the salesman who she was, and what was the periodical she wanted. He answered that she was the wife of a railway workman, that the magazine was a journal of fashions, and that the demand for such journals was large and constant among women of the wage-earning class in the town. This set me to observing female dress more closely, and it turned out to be perfectly true that the women in these little towns were following the Parisian fashions very closely, and were, in fact, ahead of the majority of English ladies belonging to the professional and mercantile classes. Of course . . . these votaries of fashion did all their own housework and looked after their own babies.

When Romance Was in Flower

When the Nineties began, the romantic tradition in literature was dominant, and in the United States its leading exponent was the European-educated novelist F. Marion Crawford, who in 1893 offered to explain his art in The Novel: What It Is:

. . . It seems to be true that if the people who talk about schools of fiction mean anything or wish to mean anything, which sometimes seems doubtful, they mean this: the realist proposes to show men what they are; the romanticist tries to show men what they should be. . . . For my part, I believe that more good can be done by showing men what they may be, or can be, than by describing their greatest weaknesses with the highest art. We all know how bad we are; but it needs much encouragement to persuade some of us to believe that we can really be any better. To create genuine interest and afford rest and legitimate amusement, without losing sight of that fact, and to do so in a more or less traditional way, seems to be the profession of the novelist who belongs to the romantic persuasion.

. . . The prime impulses of the heart are, broadly speaking, the same in all ages and almost in all races. The brave man's beats as strongly in battle to-day, the coward's stands as suddenly still in the face of danger, boys and girls still play with love, men and women still suffer for love, and the old still warn youth and manhood against love's snares—all that and much more comes from depths not reached by civilizations nor changed by fashions. Those deep waters the real novel must fathom, sounding the tide-stream of passion and bringing up such treasures as lie far below and out of sight—out of reach of the individual in most cases—until the art of the story-teller makes him feel that they are or might be his. Caesar commanded his legionaries to strike at the face. Humanity, the novelist's master, bids him strike only at the heart.

Crawford's suggestions were not wasted on Richard Harding Davis, the dashing journalist-novelist over whom all Gibson girls swooned. Here is a love scene from his novel The Princess Aline (1895):

Carlton turned and looked at her with strange wide-open eyes, as though he saw her for the first time. He felt so sure of himself and of his love for her that the happiness of it made him tremble, and the thought that if he spoke she might answer him in the old, friendly, mocking tone of good-fellowship filled him with alarm. . . .

He leaned forward with his arm along the back of the bench, and bent his face toward hers. Her hand lay at her side, and his own closed over it, but the shock that the touch of her fingers gave him stopped and confused the words upon his tongue. He looked strangely at her, and could not find the speech he needed.

Miss Morris gave his hand a firm, friendly little pressure and drew her own away, as if he had taken hers only in an exuberance of good feeling.

"You have been very nice to us," she said, with an effort to make her tone sound kindly and approving. "And we——"

"You mustn't go; I can't let you go," said Carlton, hoarsely. There was no mistaking his tone or his earnestness now. "If you go," he went on, breathlessly, "I must go with you."

The girl moved restlessly; she leaned forward, and drew in her breath with a slight, nervous tremor. Then she turned and faced him, almost as though she were afraid of him or of herself, and they sat so for an instant in silence. The air seemed to have grown close and heavy, and Carlton saw her dimly. In the silence he heard the splash of the fountain behind them, and the rustling of the leaves in the night wind, and the low, sighing murmur of a waltz.

He raised his head to listen, and she saw in the moonlight that he was smiling. It was as though he wished to delay any answer she might make to his last words.

"That is the waltz," he said, still speaking in a whisper, "that the gypsies played that night——" He stopped,

and Miss Morris answered him by bending her head slowly in assent. It seemed to be an effort for her to even make that slight gesture.

"You don't remember it," said Carlton. "It meant nothing to you. I mean that night on the steamer when I told you what love meant to other people. What a fool I was!" he said, with an uncertain laugh.

"Yes, I remember it," she said— "last Thursday night, on the steamer."

"Thursday night!" exclaimed Carlton, indignantly. "Wednesday night, Tuesday night, how should I know what night of the week it was? It was the night of my life to me. That night I knew that I loved you as I had never hoped to care for any one in this world. When I told you that I did not know what love meant I felt all the time that I was lying. I knew that I loved you, and that I could never love any one else, and that I had never loved any one before; and if I had thought then you could care for me, your engagement or your promises would never have stopped my telling you so. You said that night that I would learn to love all the better, and more truly, for having doubted myself so long, and, oh, Edith," he cried, taking both her hands and holding them close in his own, "I cannot let you go now! I love you so! Don't laugh at me; don't mock at me. All the rest of my life depends on you."

And then Miss Morris laughed softly, just as he had begged her not to do, but her laughter was so full of happiness, and came so gently and sweetly, and spoke so truly of content, that though he let go of her hands with one of his, it was only that he might draw her to him, until her face touched his, and she felt the strength of his arm as he held her against his breast.

Crawford set the style, Davis the pace, and the young, unpublished realist writers could only grit their teeth, be patient, and smile bitterly when Mr. Dooley, the creation of Chicago newspaperman Finley Peter Dunne, picked up his bar rag and gently needled the romantic concept. The following is from Mr. Dooley in Peace and in War:

" 'Tis all wrong," said Mr. Dooley.

"They're on'y three books in th' wur-ruld worth readin',—Shakespeare, th' Bible, an' Mike Ahearn's histhry iv Chicago. I have Shakespeare on thrust, Father Kelly r-reads th' Bible f'r me, an' I didn't buy Mike Ahearn's histhry because I seen more thin he cud put into it. Books is th' roon iv people, specially novels. . . . I had it out with Father Kelly th' other day in this very matther. He was comin' up fr'm down town with an ar-rmful iv books f'r prizes at th' school. 'Have ye th' Key to Heaven there?' says I. 'No,' says he, 'th' childher that'll get these books don't need no key. They go in under th' turnstile,' he says, laughin'. . . . 'Beggin' ye'er riv'rince's pardon, ye're wrong,' I says. 'What ar-re ye goin' to do with thim young wans? Ye're goin' to make thim near-sighted an' round-shouldered,' I says. 'Ye're goin' to have thim believe that, if they behave thim-silves an' lead a virchous life, they'll marry rich an' go to Congress. They'll wake up some day, an' find out that gettin' money an' behavin' ye'ersilf don't always go together,' I says. 'Some iv th' wickedest men in th' wur-ruld have marrid rich,' I says. 'Ye're goin' to teach thim that a man doesn't have to use an ax to get along in th' wur-ruld. Ye're goin' to teach thim that a la-ad with a curlin' black mustache an' smokin' a cigareet is always a villyan, whin he's more often a barber with a lar-rge family. Life, says ye! There's no life in a book. If ye want to show thim what life is, tell thim to look around thim.' "

Life, and Death

Theodore Roosevelt, at forty-one the governor of New York and a recent war hero, looked around, as Mr. Dooley suggested, flexed his muscles, and delivered a famous speech, "The Strenuous Life." It was 1899, and Terrible Teddy so concerned Republican party leaders that they commenced to bury him (they thought) in the Vice Presidency. Here is his rousing peroration:

I preach to you, then, my countrymen, that our country calls not for the life of ease, but for the life of strenuous endeavor. The twentieth century looms before us big with the fate of many nations. If we stand idly by, if we seek merely swollen, slothful ease, and ignoble peace, if we shrink from the hard contests where men must win at hazard of their lives and at the risk of all they hold dear, then the bolder and stronger peoples will pass us by and will win for themselves the domination of the world. Let us therefore boldly face the life of strife, resolute to do our duty well and manfully; resolute to uphold righteousness by deed and by word; resolute to be both honest and brave, to serve high ideals, yet to use practical methods. Above all, let us shrink from no strife, moral or physical, within or without the nation, provided we are certain that the strife is justified; for it is only through strife, through hard and dangerous endeavor, that we shall ultimately win the goal of true national greatness.

A growing roster of young American writers did not share the romantic outlook of men like Richard Harding Davis or the irrepressible Rough Rider. One was Stephen Crane, born in 1871, who published his famous Red Badge of Courage *when he was only twenty-four. He had never fought in a war, and never would, for he died in 1900; yet his was one of the most brilliant accounts of the interior horrors of battle ever written, and he left no romance in it. In the very year of T. R.'s famous speech, 1899, he published this bitter poem,* War Is Kind:

Do not weep, maiden, for war is kind.
Because your lover threw wild hands
    toward the sky
And the affrighted steed ran on alone,
Do not weep.
War is kind.

Hoarse, booming drums of the
    regiment,
Little souls who thirst for fight,
These men were born to drill and die.
The unexplained glory flies above
    them,
Great is the battle-god, great, and his
    kingdom—
A field where a thousand corpses lie.

Do not weep, babe, for war is kind.
Because your father tumbled in the
    yellow trenches,
Raged at his breast, gulped and died,
Do not weep.
War is kind.

Swift blazing flag of the regiment,
Eagle with crest of red and gold,
These men were born to drill and die.
Point for them the virtue of slaughter,
Make plain to them the excellence of
    killing
And a field where a thousand corpses
    lie.

Mother whose heart hung humble as
    a button
On the bright splendid shroud of your
    son,
Do not weep.
War is kind.

Rich Man, Poor Man

Old Andrew Carnegie, having made his pile, was engaged in the quite uncharacteristic task (for a steel master) of giving most of it away in libraries and other benefactions. In the Nineties his writings, many of them autobiographical and nostalgic for simpler times and simpler ethical systems, were compiled in a book called The Gospel of Wealth. *There is something in what he says, despite his pieties on poverty:*

You know how people moan about poverty as being a great evil, and it seems to be accepted that if people had only plenty of money and were rich, they would be happy and more useful, and get more out of life.

As a rule, there is more genuine satisfaction, a truer life, and more obtained from life in the humble cottages of the poor than in the palaces of the rich. I always pity the sons and daughters of rich men, who are attended by servants, and have governesses at a later age, but am glad to remember that they do not know what they have missed.

They have kind fathers and mothers, too, and think that they enjoy the sweetness of these blessings to the fullest: but this they cannot do; for the poor boy who has in his father his constant companion, tutor, and model, and in his mother—holy name!—his nurse, teacher, guardian angel, saint, all in one, has a richer, more precious fortune in life than any rich man's son who is not so favored can possibly know, and compared with which all other fortunes count for little. . . .

If you will read the list of the immortals who "were not born to die," you will find that most of them have been born to the precious heritage of poverty.

It seems, nowadays, a matter of universal desire that poverty should be abolished. We should be quite willing to abolish luxury, but to abolish honest, industrious, self-denying poverty would be to destroy the soil upon which mankind produces the virtues which enable our race to reach a still higher civilization than it now possesses.

The acidic Ambrose Bierce had a pithy answer in The Devil's Dictionary *for those who tried to apply Charles Darwin's theories of natural selection to economic situations; he simply paraphrased the Eighth Commandment:*

Don't steal; thou'lt never thus compete successfully in business. Cheat.

The realists took a different view from that of Carnegie and the romantics, for they had seen the seamy side of life as it actually existed, not through the misty eyes of rural memory. The practitioners of this new form of writing—Crane, Theodore Dreiser, Frank Norris, and Harold Frederic—all got their start on newspapers, where they were exposed to the same depressing social conditions that were observed by Jacob A. Riis, the crusading police reporter of the New York Sun. *What follows is from Riis's* How the Other Half Lives:

The twenty-five cent lodging-house keeps up the pretence of a bedroom, though the head-high partition enclosing a space just large enough to hold a cot and a chair and allow the man room to pull off his clothes is the shallowest of all pretences. The fifteen-cent bed stands boldly forth without screen in a room full of bunks with sheets as yellow and blankets as foul. At the ten-cent level the locker for the sleeper's clothes disappears. There is no longer need of it. The tramp limit is reached, and there is nothing to lock up save, on general principles, the lodger. Usually the ten- and seven-cent lodgings are different grades of the same abomination. . . . A strip of canvas, strung between rough timbers, without covering of any kind, does for the couch of the seven-cent lodger who prefers the questionable comfort of a red-hot stove close to his elbow to the revelry of the stale-beer dive. It is not the most secure perch in the world. Uneasy sleepers roll off at intervals, but they have not far to fall to the next tier of bunks, and the commotion that ensues is speedily quieted by the boss and his club. On cold winter nights, when every bunk had its tenant, I have stood in such a lodging-room more than once and listening to the snoring of the sleepers like the regular strokes of an engine, and the slow creaking of the beams under their restless weight, imagined myself on shipboard and experienced the very real nausea of sea-sickness. The one thing that did not favor the deception was the air; its character could not be mistaken. . . .

According to the police figures, 4,974,025 separate lodgings were furnished last year by these dormitories, between two and three hundred in number, and, adding the 147,634 lodgings furnished by the station-houses, the total of the homeless army was 5,121,659, an average of over fourteen thousand homeless men for every night of the year! . . . More than half of the lodging-houses are in the Bowery district, that is to say, the Fourth, Sixth, and Tenth Wards, and they harbor nearly three-fourths of their crowds. . . . Appropriately enough nearly one-fifth of all the pawn-shops in the city and one-sixth of all the saloons are located here, while twenty-seven per cent of all the arrests on the police books have been credited to the district for the last two years.

The distance between the Bowery and Central Park South was measured in social light-years, which Theodore Dreiser made clear in Sister Carrie:

At Fifty-ninth Street and Fifth Avenue a blaze of lights from several new hotels which bordered the Plaza Square gave a suggestion of sumptuous hotel life. Fifth Avenue, the home of the wealthy, was noticeably crowded with carriages, and gentlemen in evening dress. At Sherry's an imposing doorman opened the coach door and helped them out. . . .

In all Carrie's experience she had never seen anything like this. . . . There was an almost indescribable atmosphere about it which convinced the newcomer that this was the proper thing. Here was the place where the matter of expense limited the patrons to the moneyed or pleasure-loving class. Carrie had read of it often in the *Morning* and *Evening World.* She had seen notices of dances, parties, balls, and suppers at Sherry's. The Misses So-and-so would give a party on Wednesday evening at Sherry's. Young Mr. So-and-so would entertain a party of friends at a private luncheon on the sixteenth, at Sherry's. The common run of conventional, perfunctory notices of the doings of society, which she could scarcely refrain from scanning each day, had given her a distinct idea of the gorgeousness and luxury of this wonderful temple of gastronomy. Now, at last, she was really in it. She had come up the imposing steps, guarded by the large and portly doorman. She had seen the lobby, guarded by another large and portly gentleman, and been waited upon by uniformed youths who took care of canes, overcoats, and the like. Here was the splendid dining-chamber, all decorated and aglow, where the wealthy ate. . . .

Incandescent lights, the reflection of their glow in polished glasses, and the shine of gilt upon the walls, combined into one tone of light which it requires minutes of complacent observation to separate and take particular note of. The white shirt fronts of the gentlemen, the bright costumes of the ladies, diamonds, jewels, fine feathers—all were exceedingly noticeable.

Carrie walked with an air equal to that of Mrs. Vance, and accepted the seat which the head waiter provided for her. She was keenly aware of all the little things that were done—the little genuflections and attentions of the waiters and head waiter which Americans pay for. The air with which the latter pulled out each chair, and the wave of the hand with which he motioned them to be seated, were worth several dollars in themselves....

The large bill of fare held an array of dishes sufficient to feed an army, sidelined with prices which made reasonable expenditure a ridiculous impossibility—an order of soup at fifty cents or a dollar, with a dozen kinds to choose from; oysters in forty styles and at sixty cents the half-dozen; entrées, fish, and meats at prices which would house one over night in an average hotel. One dollar fifty and two dollars seemed to be the most common figures upon this most tastefully printed bill of fare....

The tables were not so remarkable in themselves, and yet the imprint of Sherry upon the napery, the name of Tiffany upon the silverware, the name of Haviland upon the china, and over all the glow of the small, red-shaded candelabra and the reflected tints of the walls on garments and faces, made them seem remarkable. Each waiter added an air of exclusiveness and elegance by the manner in which he bowed, scraped, touched and trifled with things. The exclusively personal attention which he devoted to each one, standing half bent, ear to one side, elbows akimbo, saying: "Soup —green turtle, yes. One portion, yes. Oysters—certainly—half-dozen— yes. Asparagus. Olives—yes."

Doubleday published Sister Carrie *in 1900, on the advice of one of its editors, Frank Norris, and at the insistence of the author; but it was never distributed. Not until 1907 was Dreiser able to put his realistic epic on the market. The public, it seemed, was not ready for a novel about an unrepentant girl who sinned her way to fame and fortune—not even at a time when shopgirls received three dollars a week and were unemployable if half-starved, "as privation makes them stupid."*

Voices in the Wilderness

If writers like Riis—and social workers like Jane Addams, who opened Hull House in Chicago just before the Nineties began—spoke for the urban poor, another voice was being heard in defense of the industrial worker. The depression of 1893 had led sleeping-car manufacturer George M. Pullman to lay off over half his employees and cut the wages of the rest; but he did not lower rents on the company houses in his model company town of Pullman, Illinois. In May of 1894 his workers, who belonged to the American Railway Union, went out on strike. On May 16 the head of the union, Eugene Victor Debs, came to Pullman and addressed them:

I believe a rich plunderer like Pullman is a greater felon than a poor thief, and it has become no small part of the duty of this organization to strip the mask of hypocrisy from the pretended philanthropist and show him to the world as an oppressor of labor. One of the general officers of the company said today that you could not hold out against the Pullman Company more than ten days longer. If it is a fact that after working for George M. Pullman for years you appear two weeks after your work stops, ragged and hungry, it only emphasizes the charge I made before this community, and Pullman stands before you as a self-confessed robber. . . . The paternalism of Pullman is the same as the interest of a slave holder in his human chattels. You are striking to avert slavery and degradation.

But Eugene Debs was thrown in jail, and with the aid of federal troops and a federal court injunction, the strike was crushed. Organized labor's day had not yet come.

Meanwhile, out on the prairies, someone was speaking up for the embattled small farmer. Deeply in debt as a result of inflation, deeply distrusting city slickers and eastern "goldbugs," the farmer listened avidly to the silver-tongued voice of William Jennings Bryan of Nebraska. On July 8, 1896, Bryan electrified the Democratic National Convention—and captured the party's presidential nomination— with a speech that ended like this:

You come to us and tell us that the great cities are in favor of the gold standard; we reply that the great cities rest upon our broad and fertile prairies. Burn down your cities and leave our farms, and your cities will spring up again as if by magic; but destroy our farms and the grass will grow in the streets of every city in the country.

. . . If they say bimetallism is good, but that we cannot have it until other nations help us, we reply, that instead of having a gold standard because England has, we will restore bimetallism, and then let England have bimetallism because the United States has it. If they dare to come out in the open field and defend the gold standard as a good thing, we will fight them to the uttermost. Having behind us the producing masses of this nation and the world, supported by the commercial interests, the laboring interests and the toilers everywhere, we will answer their demand for a gold standard by saying to them: You shall not press down upon the brow of labor this crown of thorns, you shall not crucify mankind upon a cross of gold.

William Allen White, the young editor of the Emporia, Kansas, Gazette, *took issue with the Democratic candidate:*

That's the stuff! Give the prosperous man the dickens! Legislate the thriftless into ease, whack the stuffing out of the creditors and tell the debtor who borrowed money five years ago when money in circulation was more general than it is now, that the contraction of currency gives him a right to repudiate.

Whoop it up for the ragged trousers; put the lazy, greasy fizzle who can't pay his debts on an altar and bow down and worship him. Let the state ideal be high. What we need is not the respect of our fellow men, but a chance to get something for nothing.

. . . Let's don't stop this year. Let's drive all the decent, self-respecting men out of the state. Let's keep the old clodhoppers who know it all. Let's encourage the man who is "posted." He can talk, and what we need is not mill hands to eat our meat, nor factory hands to eat our wheat, nor cities to oppress the farmer by consuming his butter and eggs and chickens and produce; what Kansas needs is men who can talk, who have large leisure to argue the currency question while their wives wait at home for that nickel's worth of bluing.

What's the matter with Kansas?

Nothing under the shining sun. She is losing wealth, population and standing. She has got her statesmen, and the money power is afraid of her. Kansas is all right. She has started in to raise hell, as Mrs. Lease [Mary E. Lease, a Populist orator] advised, and she seems to have an over-production. But that doesn't matter. Kansas never did believe in diversified crops. Kansas is all right. There is absolutely nothing wrong with Kansas. "Every prospect pleases and only man is vile."

On September 18, 1895, Booker T. Washington, principal of the Tuskegee (Alabama) Normal and Industrial Institute, spoke at the Cotton States and International Exposition in Atlanta. "It was the first time a colored orator had ever stood upon a platform before such a vast audience with white men and women," the Atlanta Constitution reported. "[It was] an event in the history of the race."

. . . To those of the white race who look to the incoming of those of foreign birth and strange tongue and habits for the prosperity of the South, were I permitted, I would repeat what I say to my own race, "Cast down your bucket where you are." Cast it down among the eight million Negroes whose habits you know, whose fidelity and love you have tested in days when to have proved treacherous meant the ruin of your firesides. Cast down your bucket among these people who have without strikes and labor wars tilled your fields, cleared your forests, builded your railroads and cities, brought forth treasures from the bowels of the earth, and helped make possible this magnificent representation of the progress of the South. Casting down your bucket among my people, helping and encouraging them as you are doing on these grounds, and with education of head, hand, and heart, you will find that they will buy your surplus land, make blossom the waste places in your fields, and run your factories. While doing this, you can be sure, in the future, as in the past, that you and your families will be surrounded by the most patient, faithful, law-abiding, and unresentful people that the world

has seen. As we have proved our loyalty to you in the past, in nursing your children, watching by the sickbed of your mothers and fathers, and often following them with tear-dimmed eyes to their graves, so in the future, in our humble way, we shall stand by you with a devotion that no foreigner can approach, ready to lay down our lives, if need be, in defense of yours, interlacing our industrial, commercial, civil, and religious life with yours in a way that shall make the interests of both races one. [At this point, Washington suddenly thrust one hand over his head.] In all things that are purely social we can be as separate as the fingers, yet one as the hand in all things essential to mutual progress.

"The Atlanta Compromise," as the militant opponents of Washington described his speech, was historically beside the point. Reconstruction had ended officially in 1877, and by the Nineties Jim Crow laws were on the books of most southern states. In 1896, the U.S. Supreme Court gave separatism the force of law with the Plessy v. Ferguson decision, which upheld a Louisiana law requiring the railroads "to provide equal but separate accommodations for the white and colored races." Here is part of the majority opinion, written by Justice Henry Billings Brown:

. . . The [plaintiff's] argument . . . assumes that social prejudices may be overcome by legislation, and that equal rights cannot be secured by the negro except by an enforced commingling of the two races. We cannot accept this proposition. . . . Legislation is powerless to eradicate racial instincts, or to abolish distinctions based upon physical differences, and the attempt to do so can only result in accentuating the difficulties of the present situation. If the civil and political rights of both races be equal, one cannot be inferior to the other civilly or politically. If one race be inferior to the other socially, the constitution of the United States cannot put them upon the same plane.

The Negro's day had not yet come, either—and would not come for another sixty years.

National Identity

On May 2, 1890, Congress opened Oklahoma Territory for settlement; three years later, Frederick Jackson Turner, a Wisconsin history professor, announced in a speech to the American Historical Association that the nation's frontiers were closed:

Since the days when the fleet of Columbus sailed into the waters of the New World, America has been another name for opportunity, and the people of the United States have taken their tone from the incessant expansion which has not only been open but has even been forced upon them. He would be a rash prophet who should assert that the expansive character of American life has now entirely ceased. Movement has been its dominant fact, and, unless this training has no effect upon a people, the American intellect will continually demand a wider field for its exercise. But never again will such gifts of free land offer themselves. For a moment at the frontier the bonds of custom are broken, and unrestraint is triumphant. There is not *tabula rasa*. The stubborn American environment is there with its imperious summons to accept its conditions; the inherited ways of doing things are also there; and yet, in spite of environment, and in spite of custom, each frontier did indeed furnish a new field of opportunity, a gate of escape from the bondage of the past; and freshness, and confidence, and scorn of older society, impatience of its restraints and its ideas, and indifference to its lessons, have accompanied the frontier. What the Mediterranean Sea was to the Greeks, breaking the bond of custom, offering new experiences, calling out new institutions and activities, that, and more, the ever retreating frontier has been to the United States directly, and to the nations of Europe more remotely. And now, four centuries from the discovery of America, at the end of a hundred years of life under the Constitution, the frontier has gone, and with its going has closed the first period of American history.

The façade of rugged individualism remained in the central states; Hamlin Garland wrote about it in Main-Travelled Roads. *His long-suffering character, Haskins, has slaved for three years to reclaim the dilapidated farm he hopes to buy from Butler, the land speculator:*

"This farm is worth five thousand and five hundred dollars," said Butler, in a careless and decided voice.

"What!" almost shrieked the astounded Haskins. "What's that? Five thousand? Why, that's double what you offered it for three years ago."

"Of course, and it's worth it. It was all run down then; now it's in good shape. You've laid out fifteen hundred dollars in improvements, according to your own story."

"But *you* had nothin' t' do about that. It's my work an' my money."

"You bet it was; but it's my land."

"But what's to pay me for all my——"

"Ain't you had the use of 'em?" replied Butler, smiling calmly into his face.

Haskins was like a man struck on the head with a sandbag; he couldn't think; he stammered as he tried to say: "But—I never'd git the use—You'd rob me! More'n that: you agreed—you promised that I could buy or rent at the end of three years at——"

"That's all right. But I didn't say I'd let you carry off the improvements, nor that I'd go on renting the farm at two-fifty. The land is doubled in value, it don't matter how; it don't enter into the question; an' now you can pay me five hundred dollars a year rent, or take it on your own terms at fifty-five hundred, or—git out."

He was turning away when Haskins, the sweat pouring from his face, fronted him, saying again:

"But *you've* done nothing to make it so. You hain't added a cent. I put it all there myself, expectin' to buy. I worked an' sweat to improve it. I was workin' for myself an' babes——"

"Well, why didn't you buy when I offered to sell? What y' kickin' about?"

"I'm kickin' about payin' you twice f'r my own things—my own fences, my own kitchen, my own garden."

Butler laughed. "You're too green t'

eat, young feller. *Your* improvements! The law will sing another tune."

"But I trusted your word."

"Never trust anybody, my friend. Besides, I didn't promise not to do this thing. Why, man, don't look at me like that. Don't take me for a thief. It's the law. The reg'lar thing. Everybody does it."

. . . Haskins sat down blindly on a bundle of oats near by, and with staring eyes and drooping head went over the situation. He was under the lion's paw. He felt a horrible numbness in his heart and limbs. He was hid in a mist, and there was no path out. . . .

"Well, what do you think of it?" inquired the cool, mocking, insinuating voice of Butler.

"I think you're a thief and a liar!" shouted Haskins, leaping up. "A black-hearted houn'!" Butler's smile maddened him; with a sudden leap he caught a fork in his hands, and whirled it in the air. "You'll never rob another man, damn ye!" he grated through his teeth, a look of pitiless ferocity in his accusing eyes.

Butler shrank and quivered, expecting the blow; stood, held hypnotized by the eyes of the man he had a moment before despised—a man transformed into an avenging demon. But in the deadly hush between the lift of the weapon and its fall there came a gush of faint, childish laughter and then across the range of his vision, far away and dim, [Haskins] saw the sun-bright head of his baby girl, as, with the pretty, tottering run of a two-year-old, she moved across the grass of the door-yard. His hands relaxed; the fork fell to the ground; his head lowered.

"Make out y'r deed an' mor'gage, an' git off'n my land, an' don't ye never cross my line agin; if y' do, I'll kill ye."

Butler backed away from the man in wild haste, and climbing into his buggy with trembling limbs drove off down the road, leaving Haskins seated dumbly on the sunny pile of sheaves, his head sunk into his hands.

Two of every three Americans still lived, like Haskins, on the land, or in small towns. But the big cities had already begun to draw their millions. McTeague, the dentist in Frank Norris'

novel, conveyed something of the fascination of cosmopolitan San Francisco simply by describing the daily ritual of sidewalk life outside his office window:

The street never failed to interest [McTeague]. It was one of those cross streets peculiar to Western cities, situated in the heart of the residence quarter, but occupied by small tradespeople who lived in the rooms above their shops. There were corner drug stores with huge jars of red, yellow, and green liquids in their windows, very brave and gay; stationers' stores, where illustrated weeklies were tacked upon bulletin boards; barber shops with cigar stands in their vestibules; sad-looking plumbers' offices; cheap restaurants . . .

On week days the street was very lively. It woke to its work about seven o'clock, at the time when the newsboys made their appearance together with the day laborers. The laborers went trudging past in a straggling file—plumbers' apprentices, their pockets stuffed with sections of lead pipe, tweezers, and pliers; carpenters, carrying nothing but their little pasteboard lunch baskets painted to imitate leather; gangs of street workers, their overalls soiled with yellow clay, their picks and long-handled shovels over their shoulders; plasterers, spotted with lime from head to foot. This little army of workers, tramping steadily in one direction, met and mingled with other toilers of a different description —conductors and "swing men" of the cable company going on duty; heavy-eyed night clerks from the drug stores on their way home to sleep; roundsmen returning to the precinct police station to make their night report, and Chinese market gardeners teetering past under their heavy baskets. The cable cars began to fill up; all along the street could be seen the shop keepers taking down their shutters.

Between seven and eight the street breakfasted. . . . Everywhere was the smell of coffee and of frying steaks. A little later, following in the path of the day laborers, came the clerks and shop girls, dressed with a certain cheap smartness, always in a hurry, glancing apprehensively at the power-house clock. Their employers followed an hour or so later—on the cable cars for the most part—whiskered gentlemen with huge stomachs, reading the morning papers with great gravity; bank cashiers and insurance clerks with flowers in their buttonholes.

At the same time the school children invaded the street, filling the air with a clamor of shrill voices, stopping at the stationers' shops, or idling a moment in the doorways of the candy stores. For over half an hour they held possession of the sidewalks, then suddenly disappeared, leaving behind one or two stragglers who hurried along with great strides of their little thin legs, very anxious and preoccupied.

Towards eleven o'clock the ladies from the great avenue a block above Polk Street made their appearance, promenading the sidewalks leisurely, deliberately. They were at their morning's marketing. They were handsome women, beautifully dressed. They knew by name their butchers and grocers and vegetable men. From his window McTeague saw them in front of the stalls, gloved and veiled and daintily shod, the subservient provision-men at their elbows, scribbling hastily in the order books. They all seemed to know one another, these grand ladies from the fashionable avenue. Meetings took place here and there; a conversation was begun; others arrived; groups were formed; little impromptu receptions were held before the chopping blocks of butchers' stalls, or on the sidewalk, around boxes of berries and fruit.

From noon to evening the population of the street was of a mixed character. The street was busiest at that time; a vast and prolonged murmur arose—the mingled shuffling of feet, the rattle of wheels, the heavy trundling of cable cars. At four o'clock the school children once more swarmed the sidewalks, again disappearing with surprising suddenness. At six the great homeward march commenced; the cars were crowded, the laborers thronged the sidewalks, the newsboys chanted the evening papers. Then all at once the street fell quiet; hardly a soul was in sight; the sidewalks were deserted. It was supper hour. Evening began; and one by one a multitude of lights, from the demoniac glare of the druggists' windows to the dazzling blue whiteness of the electric globes, grew thick from street corner to street corner. Once more the street was crowded. Now there was no thought but for amusement. The cable cars were loaded with theatre-goers—men in high hats and young girls in furred opera cloaks. On the sidewalks were groups and couples—the plumbers' apprentices, the girls of the ribbon counters, the little families that lived on the second stories over their shops, the dressmakers, the small doctors, the harness makers—all the various inhabitants of the street were abroad, strolling idly from shop window to shop window, taking the air after the day's work. Groups of girls collected on the corners, talking and laughing very loud, making remarks upon the young men that passed them. The *tamale* men appeared. A band of Salvationists began to sing before a saloon.

Then, little by little, Polk Street dropped back to solitude. Eleven o'clock struck from the power-house clock. Lights were extinguished. At one o'clock the cable stopped, leaving an abrupt silence in the air. All at once it seemed very still. The only noises were the occasional footfalls of a policeman and the persistent calling of ducks and geese in the closed market. The street was asleep.

Finis

In 1897 Queen Victoria celebrated her sixth decade on the throne of England and its far-flung empire. She would reign for over three more years, but down in his Sixth Ward Chicago tavern, Mr. Dooley sensed the end of an era and paused to recapitulate:

"Great happenin's have me an' Queen Victorya seen in these sixty years. Durin' our binificent prisence on earth th' nations have grown r-rich an' prosperous. Great Britain has ixtinded her domain until th' sun niver sets on it. . . . While she was lookin' on in England, I was lookin' on in this counthry. I have seen America spread out fr'm th' Atlantic to th' Pacific, with a branch office iv the Standard Ile Company in ivry hamlet. I've seen th' shackles dropped fr'm th' slave, so's he cud be lynched in Ohio. I've seen this gr-reat city desthroyed be fire fr'm De Koven Sthreet to th' Lake View pumpin' station, and thin rise felix-like fr'm its ashes, all but th' West Side, which was not burned. I've seen Jim Mace beat Mike McCool, an' Tom Allen beat Jim Mace, an' somebody beat Tom Allen, an' Jawn Sullivan beat him, an' Corbett beat Sullivan, an' Fitz beat Corbett; an', if I live to cillybrate me goold-watch-an'-chain jubilee, I may see some wan put it all over Fitz.

"Oh, what things I've seen in me day an' Victorya's! Think iv that gran' procission iv lithry men—Tinnyson an' Longfellow an' Bill Nye an' Ella Wheeler Wilcox an' Tim Scanlan an' —an' I can't name them all: they're too manny. An' th' brave gin'rals—Von Molkey an' Bismarck an' U. S. Grant an' gallant Phil Shurdan an' Coxey. Think iv thim durin' me reign. An' th' invintions,—th' steam-injine an' th' printin'-press an' th' cotton-gin an' th' gin sour an' th' bicycle an' th' flyin'-machine an' th' nickel-in-th'-slot machine an' th' Croker machine an' th' sody fountain an'—crownin' wur-ruk iv our civilization—th' cash raygisther. What gr-reat advances has science made in my time an' Victorya's! f'r, whin we entered public life, it took three men to watch th' bar-keep, while to-day ye can tell within $8 an hour what he's took in.

"Glory be, whin I look back fr'm this day iv gin'ral rejoicin' in me rhine-stone jubilee, an' see what changes has taken place an' how manny people have died an' how much betther off th' wur-ruld is, I'm proud iv mesilf. War an' pest'lence an' famine have occurred in me time, but I count thim light compared with the binifits that have fallen to th' race since I come on th' earth."

"What ar-re ye talkin' about?" cried Mr. Hennessy, in deep disgust. "All this time ye've been standin' behind this bar ladlin' out disturbance to th' Sixth Wa-ard, an' ye haven't been as far east as Mitchigan Avnoo in twenty years. What have ye had to do with all these things?"

"Well," said Mr. Dooley, "I had as much to do with thim as th' queen."

A Boyhood in the Nineties

Reminiscences of Norwich, Connecticut

By GERARD E. JENSEN

The author of these charming boyhood stories grew up in the small but busy town of Norwich, Connecticut, which lies at the head of the Thames River, a handsome, navigable stream that made Norwich one of the early successful manufacturing towns of New England. The land had been bought long before from the Indians, and the original Uncas, whose name was taken and immortalized by James Fenimore Cooper, was the famous local chieftain. With the coming of the railroads and steamboats, Norwich began to flourish, and its inhabitants, celebrating its two-hundredth anniversary in 1859, called their hilly, inland seaport, with pardonable pride and some justice, "The Rose of New England."

My earliest memory pictures the dirt road and the horse-drawn street sprinkler slowly moving up toward our house, stirring up clouds of brown dust as the artificial rain descended from innumerable holes in the curved brass pipe at the rear of the wooden tank. Whip and reins in one hand, the driver, perched high on his narrow seat, had the other hand free to wave at little boys, barking dogs, and friendly neighbors as the chariot slowly laid a wet swath up one side of the broad street. I used to watch for the return trip, wait for the critical moment when the spray threatened to reach my toes as I sat on the carriage block, and then hastily beat a retreat.

Next door, just beyond the iron lamppost, Miss Tracy's small candy shop stood flush with the flagstone sidewalk. A vanished neighbor had once grown flowers in a greenhouse in the next yard, and the store had been his office. Now licorice passays, artificially flavored banana-shaped candies, hard candy, soft candy, and brittle coltsfoot rock rested in the windows, exposed to sun and flies. Two for a cent or five for three, as the market might run. I have since wondered how our generation survived its confections—and its staggering breakfasts.

In those days our street was used only by horses and horse-drawn vehicles—no bicycles, no automobiles. The cows went out to pasture and returned daily down the elm-shaded street. Our grocer's man came every morning in a shallow delivery wagon drawn by a brown mare. His "Whoa!" was punctuated with the snap of the hook with which he anchored the horse to the ground—a heavy iron weight on the end of a six-foot rope, with a snaffle to fasten into the ring where rein and bit met. Then came the interview in the kitchen. Seated in a kitchen chair he recited to my mother the list of his wares and took down the order for delivery later that day. In his short black reefer and black earmuff cap, Mr. Kinney was quite impressive. The pencil stuck up under the band of his headgear was always beautifully sharp, his "yesm'm's" and "nom'm's" authoritative, and his handwriting a schoolmarm's dream.

Our other daily visitor was the butcher's man, and he came perched high on the wide seat of a white delivery wagon drawn by a wiry and incredibly fleet mustang. Why Mr. Somers preferred mustangs I do not know, but I do remember their nervous starting, continuing, and stopping. In winter we boys always preferred to tie our sleds to a mustang-drawn sleigh, for only then would the wind sing in our ears as we peered cautiously through a stinging snow

ILLUSTRATED BY RAY HOULIHAN

spray, ducking the hard lumps of snow thrown from the hollows of the horse's hoofs. In summer we chose to sit beside the drivers of these remarkable steeds and survey the familiar scene from the slippery leather cushions of the open wagon, holding on to the handle at the outer edge of the seat with one hand and saluting our friends with the other.

Elms and maples, chiefly elms, lined the street and met overhead in an arch for the entire length. When I first saw them, the trees must have had all of a hundred years' growth —tall, heavily leaved, and healthy—in double rows up and down each side of the highway. We all had dense shade when we most needed it and cheerful sunlight just when it was most welcome.

In the earliest days of my youth the streets were lit after dark by gas lamps on cast-iron lampposts of simple cylindrical design surmounted by a glassed-in burner. A little boy could shin up the slippery post, catch his feet on the ridge halfway up, and just reach the button that regulated the flow of fuel. This was convenient in several ways. If the lamplighter forgot to place his ladder against the post before your house, you might be sent out to light the burner and provide the usual yellow glow that darkly lit the sidewalk for a few feet in each direction. And then there were times when one preferred the cover of darkness. It was an easy matter to extinguish the flame and no one the wiser. Even with all the posts ablaze, the street was a dark tunnel by night.

Within the dimly lit houses the lights were few and feeble. Kerosene lamps shed a murky orange-yellow light in the kitchen, the dining room, and even in the sitting room. Some kept an ornamental light in the parlor, but no one sat in that formal chamber. We read the paper and studied our books around the warm table lamp with its ivory base, white translucent shade, and double-wicked illumination. I can still smell the odor of the kerosene, and I recall the sputter of a badly trimmed wick or the singing of a lamp running low in the reservoir. The lamps were a great care, and the chore always went to the most patient and the most skillful. One had to watch the five-gallon galvanized fuel tank from which we drew our daily supplies; and there was the daily cleaning and replenishing of every lamp. Wicks always charred unevenly and had to be trimmed with sharp scissors. For the most part it was sufficient to use a burnt parlor match to rub off the sooty excess at the rim of the burner.

The street was not thickly populated, for every family needed room for a garden, a stable for the horses—usually a pair—a carriage house, and possibly a cow barn. The cow fanciers were not numerous, for it was a luxury to hire a man to take the cow to and from the distant pastureland and to provide for her milking and general care.

The prosperous families had varied and always interesting exhibits for the curious—surreys, victorias, buggies, coupés, and dogcarts. The coachmen, shaved to the quick, in uniform and hat, and smelling of saddle soap, sat erect on the box directing their carefully curried pairs, fetching and carrying their employers throughout the long hours of each day. Even in those days there were two schools of owners—those who allowed their horses to hold their heads naturally and to brandish their long tails uninhibited, and those who docked the tails and tied back the heads of their suffering beasts. Soap and leather, axle grease and dust, and the rattle of ironbound wheels, the swishing of whips, and the sharp cries of the drivers. The smell of baled hay, the sound of crunching horses, the splash of water in the washroom, rubber aprons, sponges and chamois. All the memories come back in confusion. None of us moved about very fast, but we managed to carry on the business of life without too much difficulty. The poor walked, the rich rode; but we all reached the same end at about the same time.

The World Widens

Norwich is essentially a great woods surrounded by a fringe of civilization, and every child is born on the edge of a "wilderness." Long before our formal education began, our generation went to school in our backyards and in Rockwell's Woods. Tagging at our parents' heels we learned to tell black oak from white, and both from red. We learned to recognize beech, ash, poplar, and pepperidge tree. Science was in its infancy and there came to us the early classifications of botany, the erudite story of the heavenly bodies, the dramatic history of the earth written in hill, valley, and drumlin in quartz, amethyst, and garnet. There

were birds to discover and commit to heart, and fish to call by name as they swam undisturbed by our peering eyes. Turtles and peep frogs, woodchucks and chipmunks, snakes and toads were our familiars—all the wondrous commonplaces of the freshly discovered outdoors.

A telescope in the tower of Slater Hall, at the local boys' academy, taught us what the naked eye had missed. In the basement, several immaculate plate-glass exhibition cases displayed a rich and varied collection of native Indian relics—arrowheads, adzes of stone, and other utensils and weapons surviving the Mohegans and, farther afield, the Pequots and the Niantics. In that exhibition room we learned for the first time that the ancestors of the unwarlike half-breeds we knew were men of a superior sort. It was a luminous and romantic experience. Science had provided abundantly in laboratory and showcase the rudiments of a newly discovered world.

As the son of one of the professors, I had unusual privileges that most of the small boys did not have. I often watched my father heat up the assay furnace in our cellar to test out some freshly mined ore, and there were many times when the Law brought to the school laboratory the stomach of a dead horse or cow to undergo the chemical scrutiny of my poison-hunting father. I was in on these adventures, too, as a kind of chemist's devil. My reward was often a too-long-deferred purchase of new shoes or a new suit of clothes.

There were very few doors that were shut to us boys. Once, I remember, the entire gang wheeled out to East Great Plain (really west and not very great) to watch a few laborers uncover a cluster of skeletons of Indian braves sitting under a gravel mound near the Fair Grounds. Each boy took home a bone as a relic and as another addition to his rapidly growing collection of museum pieces.

Every boy who was worth his salt had other inheritances. Industry—with a capital *I*—surrounded him, the trolley came past his door, and the firehouse was only five minutes' run from his corner. And we all knew the password. Every one of us had a rawhide whip made from the lacings of long leather belts made in nearby Greeneville and grape-vined out by the son of the "super." Now and then in the course of our wanderings in search of knowledge we dismounted at the door of the belt factory and peered in the open doorway, level with our shoulders, to catch sight of the great strips of odoriferous leather slowly shaping into mahogany-colored belts of all lengths and widths. It seemed a dull business, but when we saw the great belts rhythmically flicking and flapping a whole mill full of machinery into life we became aware of the nice workmanship that made it

possible to convey power from pulsating reciprocating engines to shafts and pulleys and machines.

One of our pals was Art Brown, the son of the super of the Falls Mill on the little Yantic River. On rare occasions he led us into the spinning room to watch the twisting of cotton yarn into endless yards of thread, and there we gazed spellbound. All deft mechanisms, however simple their end, seemed to us magical. The complicated process of weaving cotton was plainly visible through the windows of the vast Ponemah Mills on the shore of the Shetucket, another local stream; in Yantic the woolen mill exhibited the same process with a softer and more glossy material. But we boys were much more interested in the foundry belching forth great tongues of flame and reeking of stale beer and heated sand. Peering down through the gratings of the windows, we watched grimy workmen using patterns to mold sections of furnaces and radiators, and then pour red-hot iron into the flasks. It was hot and dazzling but infernally intriguing for us boys.

When all else palled, we youngsters could choose the steamboat landing, or the roundhouse, or finally the firehouse to absorb our curiosity. At home we set up electric batteries, strung telegraph wires, learned the code, and sent and received our immature communications. We learned by seeing and by doing. No school routine could ever possess the spontaneous charm of those extracurricular adventures.

Formal school came naturally enough, in an old-fashioned frame schoolhouse with rooms for eight grades and kindergarten. In the playground a high board fence separated the girls from the boys, and on our side I fought my first and only battle, with the son of our iceman. He was dark, the son of a Negro with Indian blood married to a white woman of Irish descent. He fell afoul of me in some way and, responding to the taunts of the rabble, attacked me suddenly but not unexpectedly. I was ready for him, but I think he would have done me in had his off foot not slipped at the moment when I landed a punch on his manly chest. Down he went, and I marched away victorious. Colored pupils were not numerous in those days and for that reason there was no one to root for Willie. The sympathy of the onlookers was solidly for the upper dog.

The Free Academy—our high school—in those days was a two-winged Norman structure in ugly painted brick with natural brown sandstone trimmings. It was meant to house about two hundred pupils. The boys had their side, and the girls theirs, throughout the building—even in the large assembly hall. On entering we had a choice between two courses of study—the college preparatory and the business, or general, course. Only a few of the group planned to enter college. I chose Greek and Latin and ancient history, on the road to college. In that era the teachers were born rather than made, and they were amiable souls—the sons and daughters of parents not unlike our own, and unmistakably Yankee. We boys and girls were of many sorts and descents, but mostly of native stock. The names were often the only clue. There were a few, like myself, of mixed descent. The others were the American-born offspring of German, Irish, Scandinavian, and French-Canadian parents. I recall one Armenian, born across the water, several Jewish children of various nationalities, but not one child of Italian descent.

In those days the Irishmen did the heavy manual labor of the community, the Canucks worked in the mills, the Swedes performed menial tasks in the households or in the stables, the Germans made our boots, upholstered our furniture, and supplied our delicatessen. Their children went into similarly humble occupations, but those of us natives who held our heads too high lived to see the day when the grandsons and granddaughters of these immigrants took over the destinies of the city and began to occupy the handsome old dwellings of our Yankee forebears.

Barrel Burning

In the era when the old-fashioned wooden flour barrel stood in every pantry we boys celebrated every Thanksgiving night with a barrel-burning competition, with rival pyres visible in every part of the city. That age produced several kinds of combustible barrels in all sizes—sugar barrels, flour barrels, soap barrels, and hogsheads that had once carried china from the Orient, not to mention rum from Jamaica and other inflammables. The contending gangs of boys of all ages worked for long months preceding the great day, gathering barrels and hiding them away in cellars and barns until they should be wanted for burning. We begged,

stole, and forcibly took from other boys, in the open or under concealment of darkness. Feeling ran high, and fierce struggles between gangs were not uncommon. The gangs gathered in literally *all* the wooden barrels in the city, including those in current use for ashes and trash in every family. As the season wore on and wooden boxes began to line the streets on collection day, we knew that

we had done our work thoroughly, and we respected the sanctity of these substitute containers, for we were good sports. (We had another, more selfish reason too, of course: although pine boxes are ripe for burning, we boys wanted barrels, and nothing else would do.)

On the barrel-burning day we set up a pole—a small tree freshly cut in the nearby woods, with its branches carefully removed—and over the top we slipped the bottomless barrels, one resting on top of the other until the last one hung precariously at the tip of the twenty-foot pole. That was only the beginning. At the base we then set a triple foundation of large barrels for a pyramid rising as high as our supply of smaller barrels would permit. Excelsior was then stuffed into the center of the foundation, work was stopped, and after setting a guard we boys moved on to other pursuits, including Thanksgiving dinner very late in the day. The evening fell early, and the pyres were ignited at the first sign of darkness in the western sky. We gathered in a circle around our fire, absorbed for the moment in its glory, but then we would begin to draw back and look about for signs of bigger and better fires in the other regions. Opinions differed while the flames rose high into the heavens. Norwich, being a city on several hills, lit its Jail Hill barrels last, and those in the valleys first, and one by one the columns of flame began to illuminate Lanman Hill, Plain Hill, Wawecus Hill. The sky was lurid with orange flames and smoke for a good hour—then the illumination began to die down and all that remained were heaps of red charcoal that glowed all night and still smouldered in the early morning of the next day.

How this celebration started I have never known, but I presume that it was a perpetuation of some early custom in our local history. The Indians of colonial days used fire for signalling, and our ancient mariners built fires on beaches and headlands for various purposes; we boys celebrated solely for the fun of gathering, stringing, and burning the barrels. This generation burns no more. Wood is scarce, barrels and boxes are made of other materials, and excelsior is as rare as the cardinal flower. We still waste our resources, heaven knows, even more prodigally; but the law of supply and demand and a nice little bit of technological evolution have inexorably put an end to barrel burning.

The Captain

Old Cap Stoddard lived with Mrs. Adams, widow of a bone merchant, at the corner of Warren and Franklin, just above my grandfather's house high on the bank over the street. Mother's father had once operated the local steamboat line, but he was partly paralyzed in those days and had to sit around all day doing nothing but thinking. His speech was almost incoherent, for his tongue, like his legs, wasn't under control. Visitors were always a welcome diversion—especially Captain Stoddard. His were regular, daily, morning calls that lasted well into the noon hour; the old captain was glad to find a ready listener. (Mrs. Adams was kind but somewhat severe, and she too liked to talk.) The Captain had the look of a seafaring man, but he might well have

been an officer in some regiment in the Civil War; no one ever informed me on this point and now it is too late to find out. His air was fierce, but his one-eyed squint was not heroic. In fact, he was a huddled-up old fellow with white hair and mustache, spry on his feet, but old and tired. A great black broadcloth suit enveloped his shapeless form and he moved along in black cowhide boots that extended halfway up his calves, the kind of footgear that Mr. Winkleman made by hand for his old customers down over Somers Brothers Market. On the level, Cap made fairly good speed; but in taking the numerous steps up to Grandfather's front door he lifted one heavy boot after the other, up one step at a time, all the while steadying himself with the iron rail that ran alongside to the very door. At the doorstep he would peer through the latticed outer door, ring the bell, and wait to be let in, wheezing away and muttering strange expletives. Sometimes Grandfather was on the porch warming himself in the summer sun, but for the most part he was in the little side room downstairs, seated in his old red leather chair by the window and handy to the built-in secretary with the drop lid.

"G'mornin', Hen," was Cap's usual greeting. He didn't stand on ceremony.

An indescribable reply from my grandfather.

"W-a-al, Hen, I'm here agin," and Cap let himself down into another red leather chair opposite his inarticulate host.

A silent response from Grandfather, his faded, half-blind eyes rolling about helplessly, his mouth shaped to utter a sound.

"Nice day, Hen."

Another attempt.

"I hear," said Cap, "I hear thet ol' man Brewster hez bought anuther hoss."

Pause.

"Got him off'n Cy Parks, up the street. One hunnerd dollars."

Silence.

Pause.

"Wouldn't o' give fifty myself. The critter wa'n't wuth thet much."

Silence.

"What d'yuh hear from Steve?"

Silence.

An attempt at a reply.

Long pause.

"W-a-al, I guess I'll be on my way, Hen, pritty soon."

Longer pause.

And so on for two or three hours.

Then the Captain would rise, pick up his cane, shake Grandfather's hand up and down.

"Sullong, Hen; see yuh termorrer."

And off he would go.

What these visits meant to my grandfather I could only guess, for there was no expression in his face, no distinct words to tell what he felt about anybody or anything. Cap came and Cap went, but so did morning and night, the meals, the cigars, the glass of toddy, and the patient old lady who watched over him twenty-four hours a day.

The Captain's face was equally inscrutable, but he was alive. And he seemed to enjoy his escape from the house up the street. I was too young to understand, but I did sense in him a sort of kindness. There was more behind these daily calls than temporary relief from the discipline of the womenfolk who surrounded him. It was as though he were thinking, "Henry is in a bad way; I'm glad to do what I can to break the monotony. Poor old Henry."

Circus Day

Almost every year in June the local billboards began to wear the lurid lithographs announcing the arrival in July of Barnum and Bailey's circus, or some other exhibit such as Buffalo Bill's Wild West Show. In those days all travelling tent shows, great and small, arrived in the same way—on flatcars in a long train bearing in large letters the names of the owners. The performers slept in special cars at the end. Barnum and Bailey's train was the longest and the gaudiest of all, and its hour of arrival was always very early in the morning—almost before sunrise.

On circus mornings I was never allowed to go down to the landing to see the train pull in, but I did rise early to watch for the long caravan drawn by magnificent horses up Franklin Street past our house. The rumble of huge wheels and the metallic sound of hubs brought up sharp against

the collars of the axles announced the coming of the trucks loaded with tent poles, stakes, canvas, and knocked-down bleachers. That was the first of the convoys. Burly drivers in wrinkled suits sat high holding great handfuls of reins as they talked to their horses. Sometimes there were as many as eight horses harnessed in tandem and two abreast in a long, undulating line. I knew that far down the street the gilded coaches covered with canvas slips were pulling up-grade to follow the first group, and I knew that this early-morning undress parade would go on for hours. Naturally, I didn't wait, but went on with the tentmakers to the circus lot up Washington Street.

A gang of surveyors had staked out the ground the day before, and the tent men knew precisely where to set up the great poles and exactly where the smaller tents were to go—the kitchen, the performers' tent, and the enclosure for the animals. As I used to see it, the process was curiously simple, yet titanic. The central section of the main tent was hoisted up the center poles and at the same time caught down around the circumference in such a fashion that the outer circle of small poles could be inserted. As the outer ring of canvas rose to its ten feet, the central section was again lifted. Then several gangs of stake drivers worked their way around the outer edge to drive home the short spiles that were used in drawing the canvas top into shape, once it had been raised to its full height in the center. That stake-driving was a show in itself. Four or five men with heavy sledges went around the clock in perfect rhythm, each catching the ironbound stake top with a good square blow, driving it at a sharp angle away from the center in what looked like a steady push into the earth. Finally all came taut, with the concave tent top diminishing in curve as the rope men drew in the slack and tied the Manila guy ropes in half hitches around the freshly driven stakes.

In the meantime the flow of lumbering carts went on without stopping. Men and women performers began to appear, and with them came the cooks with their portable kitchens and the smell of fire and cooking. The grunts of caged animals, the shouts of foremen supervising their gangs, the rattle of long boards slapped down on frames to make bleachers, the clank of wheels, and the hum of voices. Breakfast and a pause for all. We children took the hint and moved homeward to confound our parents with tales of great wonder. We ate. There was talk of a parade to come and a performance at two o'clock sharp. The parade was paramount, the performance a matter of indifference. *Our* circus was a moving spectacle, a pageant of power and ingenuity. The parade at eleven o'clock was for us the real show, the real climax. Then for the first time did the rest of the company of supermen make their dramatic appearance—the lion tamer, the master of ceremonies, the acro-

bats, the queenly damsels, the mounted horsemen, the ponderous animals moving along on foot, the clowns, the bandsmen, and the regal calliope player. Strength and skill were what we boys admired—not showmanship. We had viewed the real drama of circus life, we had taken in a free show of the first quality, and all else was of no consequence. When we had seen the parade we had seen all.

Nowadays it is another story. Caravans of auto trucks, power hoists, power-stake drivers—nothing human except the men seated at the steering wheels or operating portable machinery—unglamorous men and women in a mechanical routine of unromantic activity. Bored keepers, jaded animals, unhappy clowns, canned music from loud-speakers, and an automatic electric calliope. Were he alive today, Barnum, shrewd as he was, would turn away sorrowfully.

A Spring-water Route

The nabobs had their own private pipelines carrying spring water a good mile down from the woods, but the ordinary folk drank city water. Most of the old wells had been boarded over, and the old pumps had gone to the junkman. My business venture started one fall when the reservoir water was unusually muddy and unpalatable. Father assured us that the water was entirely harmless. Mother drank it with a wry face. I thought of the spring up the road in Rockwell's Woods, of the empty Poland Water bottles in our cellar, and of the soapbox cart with metal wheels on the back piazza.

"It's the algae," said Father.

"Algae or no algae," said my mother, "I'd like a glass of cold spring water right now."

"I'll get you some, Ma," I piped up.

Mother and Father exchanged glances and Father replied, quick as a flash, "Where?"

"Up in Rockwell's Woods, near the slippery-elm tree."

"Are there bottles—clean bottles?" asked my father.

"Six of 'em," said Mother, "down in the darkroom by the feed bin."

The grating of the metal tires on the tar walk and the rattle of empties announced my setting forth.

"Rinse 'em out well," called Father. "And don't fill 'em too full. If you do, you'll lose your corks."

Down the street, up to the left, and into the woods for a long uphill pull to the spring and its cast-iron faucet. The whirr of spokes in the soft earth, the singing of crickets, and the distant cawing of crows. No one in sight. Then a macadam road with a layer of loose stone. Then the turn and the sudden view of a raised terrace held together by a low stone offset wall. A few stone steps up to the dripping faucet with its great wheel. Six two-quart bottles to be filled to the neck and rinsed spotless and sweet. None of today's sterile steam baths, just cold, clear spring water and plenty of shaking. Then the filling—each bottle falling into its place with a heavy thud. And then the trip home—downhill all the way until the tires fairly rang.

"Ah-h-h!" said Mother, downing a glass in one drink, "*that's* water!"

"Not so bad," said Father. "Did you . . .?"

"Yes I did, twice," I replied.

"Can you spare another glass?" said he, with a seraphic grin.

My parents liked the crystal-clear water. It was soft and remained palatable for a long time. They spread the news. My route never had very many customers, but the ones it had were ardent devotees. With only six bottles to a load, each trip netted a very small profit for all the energy and time consumed; but there *was* a profit, and my time was not very valuable even in schooltime. The five cents I received for each two-quart bottle looked big to me. Sometimes I made two trips in one day. The technique was simple. I went to the door with my wagon load, knocked or rang, and waited for someone to respond. Usually it was the maid.

"Any water today?" I would ask.

"I'll see," was her reply.

A clinking of empties or the heavy ring of full bottles told me the answer before I could get it from her lips.

Collecting was my greatest problem. Some foresighted customers paid spot cash. Others ran up an account, and once a week I made the rounds to collect.

"Not today," was often the answer. "Mr. T—— forgot to leave the money, and he won't be back until Monday."

Mr. T—— was no manager. Mr. S—— was heedless. It was the era when no woman held the purse strings. But I got the cash eventually. You learn a lot about your neighbors when you have business dealings with them.

There were two springs from which I could draw my loads—one under the hill near the Falls Mill, the other up the golf course carry. Like most things that come too eas-

ily in life, the short and profitable trips under the hill ended abruptly with my discovery that in rainy spells the spring water was flavored with the leachings of a stable on the steep hill above.

It was mainly a summer business, for our city water tasted less strong once the pond had turned over in the early fall and cold weather was setting in. And it is as a summer occupation that I remember it best. Long, hot days with bright, relentless sun and clear blue skies. The woods were cool and delightfully hushed. In the dark recesses of what we called the "Rocky Mountains" the dew stayed late on the undergrowth. Even in the intense midday heat, black snakes liked to sun themselves on the stone walls mottled with shade and light. As I drew up to the spring the birds looked at me furtively and moved on about their business. Chipmunks and squirrels moved about swiftly and silently, half aware of my presence but mainly concerned with their private problems. Even in that recess the wild geraniums blossomed in season, the Solomon's-seal hung its berries, the jewelweed shone brightly, and up above in the brook, hellebore and skunk cabbage stood out fresh and green. Periodically there arose the shrill buzzing of locusts, and now and then the distant voices of men playing golf on the upper course at the end of the carry. And very far off, the whirr of a mowing machine and the imperative "git ap's" and "whoa's" of the farmer addressing his pair from the perforated cast-iron seat. Even more distant were the faint sounds from the city—the steamboat whistles, the clang of engine bells, and the striking of the City Hall clock.

I knew every inch of those woods. Up above me lay the covered springs of the rich families in the city and the purple trillium that loved the dark recesses near the spring-houses. A nest of copperhead snakes lay somewhere in the rocks to the left of the path that led to the top of the hill. A slippery-elm tree stood nearby, ready to supply me with my morning chew. As I filled my bottles the concerns of the moment would run through my conscious mind; in the background of half-shaped ideas lay past experience and the small, homely wisdom that came with it. And as I turned about to start downhill there was always the view: a winding road lined with great trees leaning over toward each other across the road, a great patch of blue sky overhead, and the bright spire of St. Patrick's Church piercing the sky and the clouds. Then my eye would catch sight of the gray stone Rockwell house in the meadows, and beyond that the roofs of the houses in my neighborhood. Hills to the right and to the left shut in the view, but above all emerged the cross on the church spire and the endless sky. I went to get spring water, but what I really found was something that does not evaporate—something that is not consumed in the drinking. The hurricane of 1938 took away the trees—but not my memories.

Gerard E. Jensen is professor emeritus of English at connecticut College in New London, Connecticut, only a few miles from Norwich. He has taught at Yale, Cornell, and Pennsylvania and published several books, among them a study of the nineteenth-century editor and poet H. C. Bunner. He is also the father of the editor of this magazine.

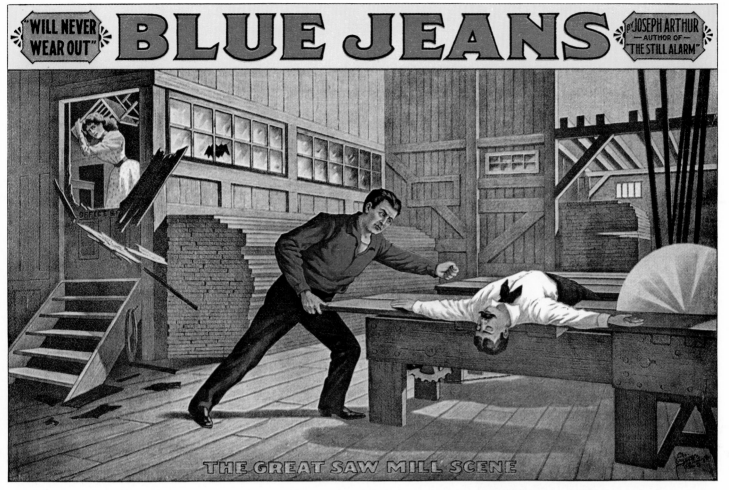

"WILL NEVER WEAR OUT" **BLUE JEANS** *By* **JOSEPH ARTHUR** —AUTHOR OF— **"THE STILL ALARM"**

THE GREAT SAW MILL SCENE

An 1890 poster depicts the climax of the hit play Blue Jeans. *The hero, though soon to be saved by his sweetheart, is menaced by a real, operating buzz saw, a touch of stage gadgetry that thrilled audiences of the day.*

Innocent Merriment (more or less)

Rags were royal raiment when worn for virtue's sake, but diamonds were moving briskly too

By HEYWOOD HALE BROUN

For more than two hundred years Americans had followed their stars to the frontier, and now in 1890 the stars were directly overhead and there wasn't any frontier any more. Frederick Jackson Turner analyzed this state of affairs in a brilliant essay, and Diamond Jim Brady considered one aspect of it very simply. "Hell, I'm rich," said Jim in the early Nineties. "It's time I had some fun."

Few Americans were as rich as Jim, but there were uncounted pokes full of gold dust, bales full of beaver skins, barns full of wheat, and banks full of money. And there wasn't any Internal Revenue Service to spoil the fun. What had been called idleness was now called leisure, and the semantic shift sent tremors through the whole structure of American life. The puritan drum-beat to which Americans had marched from Plymouth to the Pacific was to be drowned by the brass-band sound of a nation on a spree. The preoccupation with pleasure produced the Star, who provided pleasure, and the Celebrity, who conspicuously took it. You found these persons, for example, taking over the stage. Edwin Booth, whose somber majesty typified the on-ward and upward theatre of the seventies and eighties, opened what was to be his last season in March of 1891. The newspapers were unkind, his co-star Lawrence Barrett died, and on the twenty-eighth Booth said fare-

New York's leading man about town, Diamond Jim Brady, above, supplied equipment to railroads and gave extrava-gant gifts to friends, notably to "The American Beauty," Lillian Russell, the operetta star from Iowa, shown opposite at a well-upholstered thirty-one. Jim did not shoot the tiger.

well to Manhattan with what a critic mournfully called "the last great Hamlet New York ever saw." He had no real successor as a classic actor; there were, however, Personalities—alas, we have them yet—for whom could be created the kind of play that is called a Vehicle.

Perhaps the first of the Personalities was John Drew. For thirteen years he had been leading man in Augustin Daly's great stock company, playing opposite Ada Rehan. Unlike a star, a leading man does not pick his roles, talk back to his director, get preferential treat-ment, or make a great deal of money. Then one day in 1892 Charles Frohman offered all these perquisites to Drew, and the "matinee idol" was born. What the public wanted in the Nineties was spectacle and gaiety and charm. One would not have thought of calling Edwin Booth charming, but Booth Tarkington, an admirer of Drew's, admitted that "John Drew would play Simon Legree into a misunderstood gentleman."

Drew's leading lady when he left Daly was Maude Adams. William Winter was to say of her Juliet: "Many schoolgirls with a little practice would play the part just as well—and would be just as little like it"; but then Winter was to write later that "the theatre has fallen into the clutches of sordid money-grubbing trades-men, who have degraded it into a bazaar." He didn't want to have any fun. Frohman knew better than Winter what was wanted. He told his beautiful new leading lady, "If you can make the young man 'out front' wish he were the hero and the young girl sitting beside him the heroine, you can be quite sure your play will succeed."

The formula does not really fit Hamlet, but Hamlet was gone with Booth, and when Maude Adams made her debut with Drew in *The Masked Ball* in October of 1892, the critic for *Harper's* said, "It is difficult to see just who is going to prevent Miss Adams from becoming the leading exponent of light comedy in America." A few years later, when she played in J. M. Barrie's *The Little Minister*, she was the single most beloved figure in the American theatre. "Hers is the popularity of the woman even before the artist," wrote Acton Davies. "In all probability Miss Adams is as ignorant as anyone else of the secret of this spell."

Typical of the change of theatrical emphasis were the *Uncle Tom's Cabin* shows that had started in the grim realities of 1852. With the passage of years, the play's original purpose was forgotten, leaving only the melodrama. There were between four and five hun-dred "Tom shows" crisscrossing the country in the Nineties, but the crack of Simon Legree's whip was now almost drowned by the calliope. Al W. Martin, whose show was "Too Big for Imitators—Too Strong for Rivalry," got things going in each new town with a parade including:

A Lady Zouave Drum and Bugle Corps, 18 Real Georgia Plantation Shouters, Mlle. Minerva's New Orleans Creole Girls' Fife and Drum Corps, The "Original Whangdoodle Pickaninny Band," Eva's $1,500 Gold Chariot, A Log Cabin, Floats, Phaetons, Carts, Ornate Banners, Dazzling Harnesses and Uniforms, 3 Full Concert Bands, the Drum Major, an 8-Foot Colored Boy, 10 Cubans and Russian Ferocious Man-Eating Hounds, 25 Ponies, Donkeys, Oxen, Mules, Horses and Burros, All Trained as Entertaining Tricksters.

The only things not mentioned in this staggering panorama are Harriet Beecher Stowe and the actors.

Tom show actors, however, did benefit largely from a piece of symbolic logic. When the Barnum circus merged with the Bailey show, the combined operation was continually advertised as "Two shows for the price of one," and some now-unknown thinker decided, on that account, to send out a double-cast Tom show. These two-for-one operations soon caught on and became common. Sometimes two Topsies alternated the lines, or one sang while the other played the banjo, and sometimes two Legrees simultaneously whipped a pair of Uncle Toms. At the last gasp of this perverted ingenuity, a show was going about the country announcing that it had *three* Little Evas. This seems as far as the embarrassment of riches was allowed to go, but the point of all the changes, in process of which, incidentally, the Negro evolved from slave to stereotype, was to perform the remarkable feat of transforming a reformist tear-jerker into a "laff riot" without disturbing the scaffolding. If, like Diamond Jim, you wanted to have some fun, you could have it at the show that a quarter-century before would have made you cry—or enlist in the Union army.

Such was the craze for bigness that John Stetson, a Boston manager, discontented with the thin look of a Last Supper tableau in a biblical play he was staging, overruled his stage manager's reminder that there had been only twelve Apostles with the cry, "I know what I want! Gimme twenty-four!"

John L. Sullivan, who did a stretch as Simon Legree, put it this way: "In 1900 I was starring in *Uncle Tom's Cabin* with some bloodhounds. Me and the dogs give hundreds of audiences their money's worth of noise."

Certainly John L. gave the whole country its money's worth of theatrics in the years leading up to his engagement to co-star with the dog pack, and the fight in which he lost his title to Jim Corbett was the first on record in which a pair of leading actors fought for a championship. Indeed, theatrical producer William A. Brady, who managed Corbett and had already cast him in a small part or two, thought of winning the crown as principally of publicity value for Corbett's coming appearance in *Gentleman Jack,* the play spe-

Frank Mayo peering west in Davy Crockett

Maxine Elliott, poised and regal backstage, became a favorite of Edward VII.

Maude Adams playing Suzanne in The Masked Ball, *1892*

When Henrik Ibsen's play Ghosts *was staged in New York in 1894, a reviewer termed it "nauseous offal." Playgoers preferred gaiety, charm, and artifice. Their adored favorites were the winsome Maude Adams and her leading man, John Drew. Even Mayo's Davy Crockett was a rough-hewn gentleman. For realism, audiences turned to the plays of David Belasco, with their minutely realistic sets, and to the pioneering performances of William Gillette, who introduced a restrained, natural acting style.*

David Belasco—actor, producer, star-maker—affected clerical garb.

Comic DeWolf Hopper in a burlesque opera, Clover

William Gillette as a trapped spy in Secret Service, *1896*

Miss Adams with John Drew, the first matinee idol, in The Butterflies. *Right, William Farnum as Ben Hur.*

Richard Mansfield as the ineffable dandy Beau Brummell, 1890

cially written for him that was climaxed with a big boxing scene.

Sullivan, the more experienced actor as well as the more experienced fighter, had already done New York and extensive road tours in *his* specially written play, *Honest Hearts and Willing Hands,* which featured a big scene of the champion actually making horseshoes on the stage. Since fighters are often better horseshoers than they are actors, a forge was also the big prop in *The Honest Blacksmith,* the play in which Bob Fitzsimmons toured after taking the championship from "Gentleman Jim" Corbett. Fitzsimmons, who had been a real blacksmith before going into the ring, used to get carried away with nostalgia during his anvil scene

and make an occasional extra shoe as a souvenir for a friend in the audience; but both Corbett and Sullivan took their acting very seriously.

"I don't want to appear egotistical," John L. told an interviewer, "but I hope some day to be as great an actor as Booth. . . . I've just begun the business now, and of course I'm not up on all the points; but they'll come along all right. . . . None of the great actors required to study much."

It must be said for Sullivan that the points came along in time for his greatest dramatic scene, the speech to the crowd after he lost his title in New Orleans. After the knockout count he dragged himself up on the ropes and cried out to the stunned multitudes,

Daring young ladies with hourglass figures, left, swing on the flying trapeze, or so a Nineties poster proclaims. Beauties in the same ample mold, above, frolic demurely in another advertisement. Below, a more rugged lady helps Jesse James foil the law in a poster of a scene from the decade's durable favorite.

"All I have to say is that I came to the ring once too often, and if I had to get licked, I'm glad it was by an American. I remain yours truly, John L. Sullivan."

It wasn't quite up to the kind of thing Booth got to say, but its ringing simplicities were just right for the decade that cherished the line from a now-forgotten play, "Shake the hand that shook the hand of John L. Sullivan"; that loved to hear Marie Dressler sing "Heaven Will Protect the Working Girl" and to watch plays like *Blue Jeans,* in which the hero, with none of Hamlet's doubts or Sophocles' tragic flaws, grappled with the problem of escaping from being carried into a buzz saw. *Blue Jeans,* which was first played at the Fourteenth Street Theatre in New York in October of 1890 and eventually in a host of American cities, was a typical if not distinguished example of what the theatregoers were demanding. To begin with, it had that spectacular gimmick—the marching buzz saw. (Boston, in a play called *The Run of Luck,* had the first treadmill for horses on the stage, and E. Berry Wall, King of the Dudes, was among the socialites who, on opening night, sat on top of the coach that rattled along without leaving center stage.) Secondly, *Blue Jeans* celebrated rural virtues as opposed to city-slickery. This theme, to be repeated many more times, seemed to please everyone, making country people feel complacent and city people feel glamorous; both groups besieged the box office. It was the kind of simple-minded sentimentality that gives rise to popular songs, in this case, "The Picture That's Turned Toward the Wall." It was, in short, just the thing for a nation taking its first long vacation.

Entertainment theatre is "star" theatre, and there weren't enough stars available for all the things that were going to be put on in the Nineties. Fine actors aren't always stars. Many of them lack that inexplicable amalgam of arrogance, spontaneity, and excitement that marks the star personality.

Still filled with a Daly-inspired sense of propriety, John Drew once rebuked one of those new press-agent fellows for giving details of his personal habits to a newspaperman. "How on earth can it interest the public," growled Drew, "to know that I eat ham and eggs

John L. Sullivan, heavyweight champion of boxing, left, strutted into the Nineties as the unbeatable "Boston Strong Boy." A familiar of Presidents and prelates, Sullivan shocked the nation in 1892 by losing to "Gentleman Jim" Corbett. Well-shaped Anna Held, opposite, became famous in 1896 when Florenz Ziegfeld, Jr., who had imported her from Paris as a singer, broadcast a story that the nineteen-year-old French girl bathed daily in milk. The dairy tale overshadowed any musical talent she might have had.

for breakfast? It doesn't interest me unless I happen to be particularly hungry; and it certainly can't bring any money into the house. No one would be fool enough to buy seats for my performance in order to see a man who likes ham and eggs."

But before the century was over, thousands were to buy seats to see Anna Held's performances because they had heard that she bathed in milk. Milk-bathing is a somewhat more bizarre custom than eating ham and eggs, but no more promising of talent on the stage. It is just the sort of grandly vulgar thing that stars sometimes do, however, and Florenz Ziegfeld, Jr., who graduated from managing Sandow the Strong Man to managing and then marrying Miss Held, was to make many stars before he was through.

The managers who hired fighters to act, or tried to get Sandow to play Charles, the wrestler in *As You Like It* (Sandow refused when he discovered he would be required to lose), were transferring existing glamour to another field; but when David Belasco made a star of Mrs. Leslie Carter, he started with a lady whose only theatrical assets were bright red hair, determination, and a lot of spare time as the result of the breakup of her marriage.

The incredible Belasco had had his first play, *Jim Black, or The Regulator's Revenge,* commercially produced when he was twelve. Before he was thirty he had acted in 170 plays, directed over 300, and written more than 100. He saw the star quality in Mrs. Carter and taught her just enough acting to get by. He introduced her to the public in *The Ugly Duckling* in November of 1890, said grudgingly that her work was "crude but promising," and went back to polishing her technique. In 1895 he created a perfect star vehicle for her in *The Heart of Maryland,* a melodrama based on the old poem "Curfew Must Not Ring Tonight," in which Mrs. Carter, as a heroine bearing the inspired name of Maryland Calvert, hung from a bell clapper to stop the sound of curfew and save her lover's life. There can be no doubt that he made her a star, but contemporary opinion seems to indicate that he didn't make her into an actress. "She is as hard as an arc light," wrote Norman Hapgood, "and as lacking in exquisitiveness as a turnip." Still, the bell scene from *Heart of Mary-*
CONTINUED ON PAGE 122

The war with poor old Spain was all Galahadism, messages to García, fire-when-ready-Gridleys, and a great circulation builder for the yellow press. The inheritance, good and bad, is with us yet

A Fling at Empire

During the lazy days of late August, 1898, the American people contemplated their recent triumph with the complacent belief that the laurels of victory had been pressed on the brow of a truly deserving champion. Not only had their fight been brave, but it had been idealistic in every way. They had taken up arms with no war aims except to free the oppressed and suffering Cubans. Americans were a peaceable people, but their Spanish enemy had been a brutal tyrant who deserved the thrashing he got. And the immediate provocation that brought them to war had been one beyond enduring; no proud nation could have done anything but fight after that flaming moment when the battleship *Maine* and so many of her brave men went to their deaths in Havana harbor. Furthermore, the way in which the gods of battle had so overwhelmingly favored American arms during the war seemed proof almost positive that one's strength is as the strength of ten when one's heart is pure.

But that was a long time ago, in a less sophisticated era, when the nation could go to war for a reason as unabashedly quixotic as aiding a tyrannized neighbor. In the years since, the Spanish-American War has been pushed into the background. It has come to be considered a comic-opera kind of little war, not very dangerous, vaguely funny, and completely unnecessary.

It has become a conflict remembered as slogans and brief episodes rather than as an important period in American history. It is the message to García. It is Hearst and Pulitzer fighting for newspaper circulation with sensational (and often fabricated) stories about Spanish atrocities. It is "Remember the *Maine*." It is Teddy Roosevelt and the Rough Riders. It is Dewey at Manila Bay saying, "You may fire when you are ready, Gridley." But very seldom are these various elements put together in correct sequence and proper perspective, for most of us tend to dismiss the war as a naïve adventure, without consequences and better forgotten.

But the war was not a simple period piece as far as its ultimate effects were concerned. Although the young Americans who volunteered so eagerly in 1898 had nothing in mind beyond driving the cruel Spaniards out of Cuba, some of those same young men found themselves fighting to hold an empire that had suddenly been acquired half a world away from Cuba—and from the elm-shaded streets of home. The United States, making pious statements about its selfless intentions, was having a fling at imperialism. The aftereffects still color America's image in the eyes of other peoples, and still influence American policy.

But in August of 1898 there were no worries about empire, only the jubilation of victory. The power of ancient Spain had been humbled by the citizen-soldiers of the United States. It was a time for honoring great men, and in the next few months, before a grateful nation forgot its heroes, there was a brisk sale of such items as the commemorative color lithograph at left, which not only assembles the war's leaders but adds a chronology, snatches of "The Star-Spangled Banner," depictions of a moment of glory or two, symbolic maidens, and who knows what else that may be found in a careful search.

On the following pages are contemporary pictures of this forgotten war. The coloring of most of them is garish and the style sometimes verges on the absurd, but pictures are not war. Dying in the Spanish-American conflict was no more colorful or absurd than in any other.

In a nation bursting with patriotism and hungry for heroes, flamboyant Teddy Roosevelt and his Rough Riders were quickly idolized. Roosevelt hardly discouraged the adulation; when he wrote a book about his experiences he intimated that the Rough Riders had stormed San Juan Hill alone, and he could recall no other officer being at the crest. ". . . if I was him I'd call the book *Alone in Cubia*," said Finley Peter Dunne ("Mr. Dooley"). The above chromolithograph of the charge is pure fiction; all except officers' mounts had been left in Florida and the regiment was afoot. Above right, publisher William R. Hearst, who had gone to Cuba to see for himself the war he had so assiduously promoted, "reviews" troops moving up to San Juan Hill. The painting is by Charles Post, who was among the passing soldiers. At right, a deservedly forgotten artist proudly pictures *Our Victorious Fleet in Cuban Waters* in an impossible formation and with most peculiar perspective.

"ALONE
IN
CUBIA"

"LITTLE BROWN BROTHERS"

Cuba and the Cubans had been the cause of the war, but the first battle was fought in Manila Bay in the Philippines, another relic of the Spanish empire which no one—so far—coveted. Well, almost no one. At left, in a painting by Rufus Zogbaum, Commodore George Dewey views the action from the vantage point of the navigating bridge on his fast flagship *Olympia*. At top right, Americans advance during the siege of Manila. Actually the siege was relatively bloodless, and the capture of Manila was a mock battle designed to satisfy Spanish honor without harming anyone. To the hurt surprise of Americans, the Filipinos demanded freedom and not the status of "little brown brothers" to new masters. In 1899, insurgents began an offensive against American forces, and it continued as guerrilla warfare into 1902. At right, Filipino troops retreat in the first fighting of that long insurrection.

For weeks, during the spring and early summer of 1898, American warships had bottled up Admiral Cervera's fleet in the harbor of Santiago de Cuba. When American troops stormed San Juan Hill on July 1 and besieged Santiago by land, Cervera was trapped and expected to surrender; his superiors, safely distant, ordered otherwise. So, on the morning of July 3 the Spanish fleet steamed out with little prospect but to perish. Below, an artist visualizes the battle where, fighting bravely on decrepit ships, died the descendants of sailors of the galleons. And on the pages following is a classic account of the tragic sea battle by historian Walter Millis.

The Spanish Fleet Comes Out to Die

By WALTER MILLIS

It was a beautiful day; the early mist burned off to leave a hot and glass-like calm, with the columns of smoke standing in graceful pillars upon the still and lovely air. It was "one of those summer days when not the slightest breath of air stirs the leaves of the trees, when not the smallest cloud is visible in the skies, when not the slightest vapor fills the atmosphere, which was wonderfully transparent." Amid this placid beauty the fleet resumed the usual small businesses of the day. It was lying, as always, in a wide semicircle around the harbor entrance; Morro Castle formed its center and the radius was about four or five miles. Commodore [Winfield Scott] Schley in his armored cruiser *Brooklyn* lay nearest to the shore upon the west, but rather farther out than usual. Then came the battleships *Texas* and *Iowa*, so placed that both of them could look up the narrow gut which formed the harbor mouth. Then came the battleship *Oregon*, already famous for her long run around Cape Horn; then [Admiral William T.] Sampson's flagship, the armored cruiser *New York*, well around upon the eastern side of the arc; and finally, the battleship *Indiana*. Two converted yachts, the *Vixen* and the *Gloucester* (Mr. J. P. Morgan's *Corsair*), were stationed close inshore at the western and eastern ends of the semicircle.

Presently the flagship *New York* made ready to depart upon her mission to Siboney, seven or eight miles away to the eastward. Shortly before nine her engines were rung ahead; the customary signal "Disregard motions of commander-in-chief" was hoisted, and she left the line. Commodore Schley was informed of her departure; it may have induced a bitter thought. The Commodore ... had been smarting for a month under the orders of a former junior. Sampson had first been promoted Admiral over his head and then . . . had been placed directly in command over him. For one who had begun the war as the commander of an independent squadron, this was rather pointed. But as the flagship departed on her errand, the Commodore could at least reflect that he was temporarily the senior officer present.

The crews of the other ships watched the *New York* growing smaller in the distance, and then turned to the customary Sunday morning muster. . . . Officers and men had put on their clean white uniforms, and in the captain's cabin of the *Iowa* [Robley D.] "Fighting Bob" Evans ... was just finishing his after-breakfast cigar.

It was at this moment that a general alarm rang through the ship.

Captain Evans leapt to his feet and dashed for the companion ladder. Just as his head came even with the deck, he heard his own ship fire a signal gun; looking out, he saw, coming down the channel bow on under a full head of steam, the *Maria Teresa*, flagship of Admiral [Pascual] Cervera [y Topete]. Resplendent in the brilliant sunshine, with a new coat of paint, with the smoke pouring from her funnels, a

"bone in her teeth," and the great blood-and-golden battle-flags of Spain at her mastheads, she was heading directly for the American fleet and the open sea. Behind her, in the narrow passage between the gray heights of the Morro on the one hand and the Socapa Hill upon the other, there swung successively into view the *Vizcaya*, the *Cristóbal Colón*, and the *Almirante Oquendo*. And behind them in turn were the *Furor* and *Plutón*, Cervera's much-dreaded torpedo-boat destroyers. The Spanish fleet was coming out.

Before Captain Evans reached the bridge the signal that the enemy was emerging—in all the American ships it had been kept bent on and ready for the past month—had been hoisted and the *Iowa*'s engines had been rung full speed ahead. Similar signals were fluttering from the mastheads of the other vessels; while all, acting upon the curiously simple standing orders of Admiral Sampson, were preparing to rush forward in a converging "charge" upon the harbor mouth. Throughout the fleet the men were tumbling down the ladders to their battle stations; the fire-room crews were outdoing themselves in their efforts to crowd steam upon the boilers, while, as the ships slowly gathered headway, impatient navigating officers took notes to see who was leading in the rush.

But amid all the hurry and excitement a wonderful, an incredible truth was dawning rapidly upon a martial figure on the bridge of the *Brooklyn*.

FROM *The Martial Spirit* BY WALTER MILLIS, REPRINTED BY PERMISSION OF HOUGHTON MIFFLIN COMPANY

The supreme moment had come at last, and Admiral Sampson, by a just irony of fate, had gone to Siboney! Commodore Schley was, clearly, in command.

...About 9:35 the *Maria Teresa* opened fire at long range. Some miles away, near Siboney, the people in the *New York* heard it. Admiral Sampson looked back, and plainly saw the distant silhouette of the Spanish flagship emerging from the entrance. Admiral Sampson, too, perceived that the great moment had arrived and that he was not there. . . .

The heroic solution of a sortie had not been adopted by Admiral Cervera upon his own judgment. With the debarkation of [General William R.] Shafter's army he had come to the conclusion that it was already "absolutely impossible for squadron to escape," and, considering its naval role at an end, had put ashore his crews to assist in the land defense of the city. From the safe distances of Havana and Madrid, however, the idea of simply sitting down and permitting the squadron to fall into [U.S.] hands by capture had no attractions. Even before the assault on San Juan, the Captain-General of the island was exerting pressure upon Admiral Cervera to attempt an escape—less for any military reason, since once the squadron got out it would be as helpless as before, than because "if we should lose the squadron without fighting the moral effect would be terrible, both in Spain and abroad." The Admiral convened a board of officers, took their views, and made a gloomy and remarkable reply: "The absolutely certain result will be the ruin of each and all of the ships and the death of the greater part of their crews. . . . I, who am a man without ambitions, without mad passions . . . state most emphatically that I shall never be the one to decree the horrible and useless hecatomb which will be the only possible result of the sortie from here by main force, for I should consider myself responsible before God and history for the lives sacrificed on the altar of vanity and not in the true defense of the country."

It was a realism which did not appeal to political superiors who had their own reputations to take care of.

. . . Finally, on June 28, [Cervera] was explicitly ordered to watch for an opportunity to go out; and should none offer, he was commanded to go out anyway, when the fall of the city seemed imminent. . . .

In a few minutes the flagship had rounded Smith Key and [entered] the upper end of the long, narrow entrance channel. Some miles away, framed between the twin bluffs which had for so long protected them, they saw at last the gray hulls of the waiting battleships. The *Teresa* held her course; her consorts followed steadily in her wake. A few minutes more and the flagship had passed out between the hills into the open sea. Already the smoke was pouring in startled clouds from the funnels of the American vessels; already they were gathering way in their charge upon the emerging squadron. But the *Teresa* held onward —they could not turn west until they had cleared El Diamante, a hidden shoal lying well offshore. An absolute silence reigned, save for the pounding of the engines and the throbbing of their hearts. Presently the pilot spoke: "Admiral, the helm may be shifted now." Cervera gave the order; the wheel was put over and the *Teresa's* bow swung to the westward. A moment later Captain Concas asked permission to open fire; the Admiral assented, and the clear notes of the bugles rang through the ship.

"My bugles [said the captain afterward] were the last echo of those which history tells were sounded in the taking of Granada; it was the signal that the history of four centuries of greatness was ended. . . .

"'Poor Spain!' I said to my beloved and noble Admiral, and he answered by an expressive motion, as though to say he had done everything to avoid it, and that his conscience was clear. . . .

"The second gun of the deck battery was the first to open fire, and brought us back to this reality, too dreadful to allow us to think of other things. Giving the cruiser all her speed, we poured out a frantic fire."

Pandemonium ensued. One by one the three other cruisers came up to the Diamond Bank in her wake and swung to the westward. Each, with an as-

tounding punctilio, slowed at the turn —the most dangerous point—to drop her pilot, for the pilots were civilians. Then the American gunners began to hit; there was a melee of rushing ships and powder-smoke, and a few minutes later pursuers and pursued alike were racing westward under the lofty Cuban coast line, the sea and the inland valleys reverberating to the thunders of the cannonade. Cervera had got out.

It is clear that Admiral Sampson's naïve plan of action—to rush in and sink the Spaniards in the channel mouth—had failed. Exactly what happened in the next few minutes was obscured at the time by the powder-smoke and has been clouded ever since in the darker fogs of a famous controversy. Admiral Sampson was not present to alter his dispositions; but in the tensity of the moment it apparently did not occur to Commodore Schley to do so. Our joyously converging ships were already in danger from each other's cross-fire; while the *Brooklyn*, charging up in a northeasterly direction, found herself almost head on to the *Teresa*, and the closest of all our vessels to the Spanish fleet. The *Teresa* swung to ram, but then fell off and broke westward with her consorts. . . .

However, the American fleet eventually got itself more or less disentangled and streaming down the coast, while Commodore Schley, once more remembering that he was in command, hoisted the signal "Follow the flag," an order which was already being obeyed to the best of our captains' ability, since the flagship happened to be the nearest to the Spaniards. For a few bad moments it seemed rather doubtful whether we should overtake them. Most of our battleships had been four or five miles to the south or east of the entrance at the beginning of the action, and were being left behind. Even the *Brooklyn* was well astern of the leading Spanish ship, and the *Brooklyn* had only half her power available. Behind her the battleship *Oregon* was forging up (her commander had kept all his boilers lighted against such an emergency); but the *Texas* was already out of it, and the rest of the squadron was spread out behind, the press boats tearing along in a frenzy of excitement on the wings, while far in the rear Admiral Sampson's *New York* was laboring to catch up with the fast-vanishing battle.

And in spite of everything Admiral Cervera might conceivably have got away had it not been for one fatal weakness in his own ships. Their decks were of wood. In the whole course of the action no one of the four was vitally injured in hull or machinery, but our first hits set them on fire. The wind of their own motion quickly converted their upper works into so many furnaces, and their devoted gunners found themselves serving their almost useless batteries with the deck-planking burning away under their feet.

The *Teresa*, receiving the brunt of the American attack as she led the squadron out, must have been on fire a very few minutes after she had started westward. A shell cut an auxiliary steam line; the ship was suddenly filled with live steam, and lost speed. Another wrecked her water mains and it became impossible to fight the fire. Captain Concas was wounded. Some of their own light-caliber ammunition stored on deck began to explode in their faces; the whole center of the ship was a mass of flames and they found they could not reach the magazines to flood them. To avoid further loss of life the Admiral soon ordered her . . . beached and abandoned . . .

A few minutes later, the *Oquendo* brought up just beyond her. The *Oquendo* was the fourth ship in the column; as the *Teresa* had received the fire from our leading vessels, the *Oquendo* had received the weight of it from those rushing up in pursuit. Her decks and cabins were soon blazing fore and aft; there was fire in the after torpedo room and in the ammunition-handling rooms, where some seamen were struggling valiantly to save the magazines by putting wet bedding over the hatches. One of her own guns burst, demolished the crew and blinded the gunner; the ammunition hoists were shot away, and a shell landed on her fore turret, putting it out of action. Fighting Bob Evans in the *Iowa* was helping to pound her to pieces. "She rolled and staggered like a drunken thing," he remembered, "and finally seemed to stop her engines," but presently went ahead again. "As I looked at her, I could see the shot holes come in her sides and our shells explode inside of her." Her interior was a furnace; most of the gun crews were dead or wounded and it was useless to continue. As she took the beach, the flames burned away the flag halliards and the ensign came down. . . .

The two destroyers—uncertain quantities which had caused some trepidation in our fleet—had emerged at about ten o'clock in the wake of the *Oquendo*. They met an even quicker death. They came out just in time to receive the concentrated fire of the fleet rushing past in pursuit of the cruisers, and it "simply overwhelmed them." A large shell was seen to land in the *Furor*; there was a cloud of smoke and steam, but the frail boat kept on. The converted yacht *Gloucester* had been posted especially to deal with the destroyers; presently she got a signal to go in and she tore them to pieces with her light guns while the rest of our fleet passed on. The destroyer crews stuck to their batteries gallantly, but they had so little training, or were so much shaken, that they did not land a single hit even though the *Gloucester* closed to six hundred yards. About four miles west of the Morro, the *Plutón* was run upon the rocks and blew up; the *Furor* went out of control and began to steam in circles. Her fire ceased entirely and some one was seen to be waving a white rag on board. The *Gloucester* sent off a boat to investigate. "They found a horrible state of affairs. . . . The vessel was a perfect shambles. As she was on fire and burning rapidly, they took off the living." Presently there was a series of explosions; the *Furor* flung up her bows and disappeared. . . .

But two of the cruisers were still alive. The *Vizcaya*, the second ship in the column, had been covered by the *Teresa* and had taken little injury at the commencement of the action. But her bottom was badly fouled and she could not make speed. The *Brooklyn* soon overhauled her, and presently the *Oregon* and the *Iowa* were within range. They failed to stop her, but they smothered her batteries and set her on fire. It was enough. She could make no effective reply. The guns jammed; often they could not get the breech-blocks to close, the firing mechanism would not work or the ammunition would not go off. . . . Fires were breaking out everywhere, and the water mains had been shot away. Yet it was not until nearly noon and they were some fifteen miles west of the Morro that their last gun was put out of action. Captain Eulate made a final effort to ram the *Brooklyn*, but it was useless. Then a steampipe burst. Then something else happened—they thought it was one of the forward boilers going up, but it was probably the explosion of one of their own torpedoes, which broke up the whole bow of the ship. Captain Eulate summoned the inevitable council of war. It was agreed that they had done all they could, and she was run in and grounded upon the rocks near Asseraderos . . .

So the *Vizcaya*, also, died. But not without one triumph. It was a shell from one of her guns which, passing across the *Brooklyn*'s forecastle, decapitated a seaman standing on the deck. Save for one other man who was wounded, this was the sole casualty in the whole American fleet. Some men standing near by made to give him an immediate burial in the sea, but Commodore Schley from the bridge stayed them with a splendid gesture. "No!" he exclaimed, according to his own account, "do not throw that body overboard. One who has fallen so gallantly deserves the honors of Christian burial!" In the Spanish squadron there was less chance to be heroic. "Don't cheer, boys," cried Captain Philip of the *Texas* as his ship went by the burning wreck of the *Vizcaya*, "the poor devils are dying!" When the *Iowa* came up, Fighting Bob observed that it was useless to try to overtake the *Colón*; he stopped his engines and sent off his boats to rescue the *Vizcaya*'s crew alive from the fire and from the insurgents who were probably behind the beach. Captain Eulate was hoisted overside in a chair, "covered with blood from three wounds, with a blood-stained handkerchief about his bare head."

"As the chair was placed on the quarter-deck, he slowly raised himself to his feet, unbuckled his sword belt, kissed the hilt of his sword, and bowing low gracefully presented it to me as a token of surrender. . . . I instantly handed it back to Captain Eulate. . . . As I supported the Captain toward my cabin, he stopped for a moment just as we reached the hatch and drawing himself up to his full height, with his right arm extended above his head, exclaimed, "Adios, *Vizcaya!*" Just as the words passed his lips the forward magazine of his late command, as if arranged for the purpose, exploded with magnificent effect. . . ."

The *Colón* had gone inshore of her consorts, concealed by their smoke, and had cleared the action almost untouched. It was past noon, and to her officers it seemed that the pursuers were falling astern and the race nearly won, when she suddenly came to the end of her scanty stock of good fuel and the engine-room force had to turn to the inferior coal making up the rest of her supply. Steam began to go down, and the speed fell. About one o'clock the *Oregon* tried a ranging shot with her thirteen-inch guns; it fell short, but she tried again and presently a column of water sprang into the air beyond the *Colón*'s bows. She was within range. The *Colón*'s own heavy guns were in Genoa, and even her secondary battery could not be trained far enough aft to bear. Her disheartened commander gave up the fight on the spot. . . . the helm was put up and the *Colón* headed for the shore. The Americans held their fire, and a few minutes later the last of Cervera's squadron ran hard and fast aground. . . .

The naval battle of Santiago was at an end. But an almost equally famous battle was just beginning. It was perhaps half an hour after the *Colón* had grounded and after the *Brooklyn*'s captain had gone aboard to receive her surrender that Sampson in the *New York* finally caught up with his action. He was greeted by a significant signal from Commodore Schley's flagship: "We have gained a great victory. Details will be communicated." It apparently took some minutes for the full import of this message to sink into the Admiral's mind, but when it did, the reply was curt: "Report your casualties." . . .

"It is to be regretted," as the Com-

modore afterward wrote, "that no word of congratulation, so much valued by men and officers on such occasions, issued from the flagship." After a pause the Commodore tried again with a hopeful "This is a great day for our country." The only reply from the outraged flagship was the hoisting of an answering pennant. The *Brooklyn*'s captain, now observed to be coming away from the surrendered Spaniard, was summarily ordered to report aboard the *New York* instead of to the Commodore. The Commodore recalled that when he himself presently went to make report, the crews of all the ships there, except the *New York*, "manned the rail, shouting in tumultuous huzzas that fairly shook the air. It was a tribute of confidence, an expression of approval in the very smoke of battle that cannot be dimmed or diminished by envious disappointments shown afterwards." But on board the flagship the atmosphere of envious disappointment was already only too manifest; for his egregious subordinate's effort to take the credit on a technicality must have seemed to the Admiral an act of unparalleled impudence. Admiral Sampson received the Commodore with a chill formality, and the tension was only relieved when a sudden report that another Spanish ship had been discovered off Santiago made it possible to despatch the Commodore in pursuit.

The report, of course, turned out to be a mistake. There was a stranger, but she was a sight-seeing Austrian man-of-war; and although the enthusiasm of our victorious ships, combined with the similarity of the Austrian to the Spanish flag, nearly resulted in her destruction, the Commodore perceived in time that he had been sent off on a false alarm. But it had brought him within reach of the cable station; the Commodore saw a golden opportunity, and he hastened to prepare a telegram to Washington, reporting the victory and carrying the delicate implication that he had won it. Even here, however, the Admiral forestalled him; the officer bearing the telegram reached the cable station just behind one of Sampson's officers, and the Commodore's telegram was not sent. In the Admiral's, the Commodore was not

even mentioned. . . .

That Sunday evening had fallen in Washington upon a city exhausted by the heat and the intense anxiety. [A] nervous little group was still waiting at the White House when at seven o'clock it was thrown into dismay by a dreadful telegram from General Shafter, detailing the first reports of the naval action, but implying that Cervera had escaped. They hung over the wires. Three quarters of an hour later, there was another despatch from the Army; it was more hopeful, but the wording was ambiguous. Still later in the evening, General Shafter remembered to inform his superiors that he had demanded the surrender of the city—on top of the morning's telegram about withdrawing, it left them in a state of considerable mystification, but "the curtain of gloom was rising." It was not until one o'clock in the morning that another telegram from Shafter fully confirmed the destruction of Cervera's fleet, and fifteen minutes later that still another came, containing the single triumphant sentence: "I shall hold my present position."

As yet there was no word from the Navy, but the curtain had lifted. At two o'clock on the morning of the Fourth of July, [Secretary of War Russell A.] Alger walked homeward "with the newsboys crying in my ears the joyful tidings of 'Full account of the destruction of Spanish fleet!'"

At about noon next day, Admiral Sampson's message . . . arrived: "The fleet under my command offers the nation as a Fourth of July present the whole of Cervera's fleet. It attempted to escape at 9:30 this morning. At 2 the last ship, the *Cristóbal Colón*, had run ashore seventy-five miles west of Santiago and hauled down her colors."

It was splendid, it was unbelievable, it was magnificent. And as the nation turned to celebrate its greatest Fourth of July since the moment, thirty-five years before, when the news of Vicksburg and of Gettysburg had arrived simultaneously upon the national holiday, the earnest statesmen perceived that the war, now, really was over. They had only to hurry to collect "the outlying things," as Senator [Henry Cabot] Lodge had called them, before Spain should cave in.

On the making of splendid little wars, and of how God spoke to William McKinley about taking an empire in the Orient without fully explaining the consequences

By RALPH ANDRIST

The shining armor in which Galahad had gone forth to do battle with the dark forces of Spain began to tarnish in a short time. The pure knight had proven corruptible; the maiden in distress, Cuba, had not even been completely freed from the hand of the ravisher before her champion was feeling the urge to do some ravishing of his own. In short, the United States in 1898 had been seduced by the charms of imperialism.

The acquisitive spirit began to show itself almost as soon as Dewey had beaten the Spanish fleet at Manila Bay, and by the time the brief fighting ended three months later, the Chicago *Times-Herald,* a fairly representative spokesman for expansion, could say: ". . . We find that we want the Philippines. . . . We also want Porto Rico. . . . We may want the Carolines, the Ladrones, the Pelew, and the Marianna groups. If we do we will take them. . . . Much as we deplore the necessity for territorial acquisition, the people now believe that the United States owes it to civilization to accept the responsibilities imposed upon it by the fortunes of war."

This apparent swing from bright idealism to imperialism did not denote any sudden change in the American temperament. The nation in 1898 was bumptious, ebullient, and aggressive. It had just won a war without half trying and now felt itself the peer of world powers like Britain and France. As a world power it wanted all the perquisites—and in the era of rampant imperialism, all first-class powers had colonies. And conscience was flexible enough to dismiss any contradictions between freeing Cuba and annexing the Philippines.

The war itself had been needless. The American people had become emotionally involved in the long and destructive Cuban insurrection, with considerable help from skillful Cuban propaganda and the American yellow press, which not only often distorted events but even fabricated stories out of whole cloth. The resulting picture of brave Cubans fighting brutal Spanish suppression was not completely accurate, for the rebels were as ruthless in their methods as the Spanish, and, moreover, a great many Cubans were neutral, or loyal to Spain. Regardless, American sympathies were firmly committed to the insurgent cause.

Even so, the whole problem seemed on the way to a solution after a liberal Spanish ministry took over in October, 1897, offered Cuba a degree of autonomy, and ended some of the worst cruelties of the campaign against the insurgents. Tensions were easing when everything collapsed in one moment: on the night of February 15, 1898, the proud battleship *Maine* blew up in Havana Harbor with the loss of 260 lives. Although the U.S. government cautioned the public to reserve judgment, the judgments were immediately made. The press screamed that Spain was responsible, and a large segment of Congress chanted for war.

Six weeks later a naval board of inquiry reported that the *Maine* had been destroyed by an external explosion that had set off secondary explosions in the ship's forward magazines. The findings have since been questioned, but it was enough for the public at the time. Few stopped to ask why feeble Spain, desperately trying to avoid war, should have perpetrated such an act.

But even now the cause of peace was not irretriev-

117

ably lost. Spain moved swiftly to pacify the United States. It was prepared to offer an armistice if the insurgents asked for one, and the American minister cabled from Madrid that if only Spain were not pushed to the point of appearing to be coerced, it would probably grant all American demands, including self-government or complete freedom for Cuba.

All depended on McKinley. The President, like his Democratic predecessor, Cleveland, had been following a peace policy, and with courage he could have withstood the insistent demands for blood. He had support even in Congress, and, with resolution, McKinley could have mobilized the antiwar forces. But the President was a man without much resolution.

He was under tremendous pressure from his own party, in which Senator Henry Cabot Lodge and Assistant Secretary of the Navy Theodore Roosevelt were the most vocal of a circle of hot-blooded jingoists. On the eve of the conflict Roosevelt wrote in his diary: "The President feebly is painfully trying for peace. His weakness and vacillation are even more ludicrous than painful."

The pressure was too much for Mr. McKinley, who had also come to believe that the future political fortunes of the Republican party depended on a war with Spain. He asked Congress to intervene—to declare war —to bring peace to Cuba. "I have exhausted every effort to relieve the intolerable condition of affairs which is at our doors," he complained. Nowhere in his address except in an ambiguous sort of postscript did he hint that a day earlier Spain had given in on all demands and that there was no longer any reason for war. Congress gave him his declaration.

A year later McKinley admitted that he may have been a weak reed before the winds: "But for the inflamed state of public opinion, and the fact that Congress could no longer be held in check, a peaceful solution might have been had."

And so war came, and was won quickly and at remarkably low cost to the United States. On July 25, a few days after the fall of Santiago, the Spanish government asked for peace terms, and two days later Ambassador John Hay in London, an ardent expansionist who would soon be Secretary of State, wrote to Theodore Roosevelt, colonel of the Rough Riders:

"It has been a splendid little war; begun with the highest motives, carried on with magnificent intelligence and spirit, favored by that spirit which loves the brave. It is now to be concluded, I hope, with that fine good nature which is, after all, the distinguishing trait of our American character."

Even discounting Mr. Hay's smug pride, it had not been quite that splendid a little war. The men who fought it were often splendid, but they labored under incompetency and mismanagement. Most of the 200,000 volunteers who hurried to offer themselves were mustered into camps where neglect of elementary sanitation caused outbreaks of typhoid and other diseases. The dispatch of an expeditionary force from Tampa, Florida, to Cuba was a quartermaster's nightmare as unlabelled supplies in unmarked boxcars competed for clearance on a one-track railroad with troop trains of regiments who had not received their transport ship assignments. When these volunteers did sail, they wore woolen uniforms for use in a tropical climate; they were fed on bully beef that became a national scandal; and they were armed with obsolete rifles, using black powder, whose great clouds of white smoke made them easy targets in combat.

Only 379 men died on the battlefield or of mortal wounds, but to the end of 1898 thirteen men had succumbed to disease for every one killed in battle. Even the Navy, with its lopsided victories, had something to think about. Not only were its tactics at the Battle of Santiago something less than brilliant, but a board of officers examining the hulks of the four Spanish cruisers could find proof of only 122 hits. The American fleet had fired 9,433 shells!

Somehow, during the fighting in Cuba, the mission of rescuing the Cubans began to become less exciting. American soldiers at last linked up with the gallant insurgent army they had come to help and discovered that it consisted of barefoot men in tattered clothing. They found the Spaniards much more to their liking, and victor and vanquished fraternized as men who had fought hard and honorably against each other. They discovered common ground in their contempt for the Cubans, and at the surrender of Santiago the administration of the city was left in Spanish hands instead of being turned over to the insurgents.

Neighboring Puerto Rico was taken by an American force that was in somewhat of a hurry to appropriate the island before hostilities ended, for the enemy had already asked for terms. There was haste in the Philippines, too. Since his great battle, Admiral Dewey had held only the naval base at Cavite and had blockaded Manila—which would seem sufficient if his role was only to assist in Cuban liberation. But there were other considerations now, and the President had sent troops to the Philippines.

Dewey used the American Army forces for negotiation rather than fighting, and finally worked out an agreement with the Spanish commander in Manila. A strange, three-way charade ensued. To satisfy Spanish honor, the Navy first bombarded empty positions, after which American troops moved in to receive the surrender of the city from defenders who could now say they had capitulated only after having resisted and been overcome. But there was a problem with the Filipino insurgents, still ostensibly American allies and advancing beside American troops. They were not playing at mock warfare, and there was some brisk skirmishing between them and the Spanish, while the American command maneuvered feverishly to prevent the Filipinos from entering the city. The *insurrectos*, who had fought the Spanish for two years, on direct orders from President McKinley were kept from sharing in the occupation of Manila. The city surrendered on August 14, two days after a cease-fire had been signed in Washington. The news had not reached Manila because the cables were cut.

In April, when the bands had played "When Johnny Comes Marching Home," the boys had marched off with no other purpose than to free Cuba. Now, less than four months later, it was over, and they had made the United States a world power with its own colonies. It was exhilarating. It was wonderful. National spirits had seldom soared so high.

McKinley had given his terms to Spain: Cuba to be ceded at once, Puerto Rico and one of the Ladrone Islands (it would be Guam) to be given to the United States, the city and bay of Manila to be American-occupied, and the disposition of the rest of the Philippines to be decided at the peace conference.

In the Philippines, as in Cuba, an insurgent organization had fought Spain and had proclaimed itself the rightful government. It would seem that simple analogy would have called for a republic there, too. But simple reasons were no longer valid. The islands had come to represent naval bases, markets, a thumb at the nose toward Germany and Japan, which were also eyeing them. Most of all they meant more prestige in the nation's new venture into imperialism. Although highly articulate forces argued that gathering an Oriental nation to our Anglo-Saxon bosom would be a thing entirely new in American history, the atmosphere of the time was an imperialistic one and the islands were annexed. A year later Mr. McKinley told a group of churchmen how it was God who had made up his mind for him when he was distraught over whether to turn the Philippines free, or to take part or all of the islands. God had told him that "there was nothing left for us to do but to take them all, and to educate the Filipinos, and uplift and civilize and Christianize them, and by God's grace do the very best we could by them . . ." McKinley's God was not aware that the Filipinos were being Christianized before the Pilgrims landed.

The Filipinos had no wish to replace Spain with a new master, however benevolent, and in February of 1899 they rose in revolt. After being defeated in open battle, they continued until 1902 a guerrilla warfare that brought almost seventy thousand American troops into action at one time against them and cost hundreds of American lives. During the campaign the Army used many of the same methods, including torture, that we ourselves had condemned.

In 1898 Hawaii was also annexed, and tiny Wake Island was taken in. The next year the United States gained part of Samoa in a three-way bargain with Germany and Great Britain. And in 1900, during the Boxer Rebellion, the United States, that old China hand, took a prominent part.

Cuba was not at once turned over to the insurgents, who everyone had once agreed represented the rightful government. The United States managed affairs until 1902, then surprised those who expected annexation by stepping aside for the Cubans. But elsewhere in the Caribbean imperialism burgeoned. To dig a canal, Theodore Roosevelt, now advanced by McKinley's assassin from Rough Rider's saddle to President's chair, gave tacit encouragement to a revolt in Panama. In the decades that followed, intervention became a normal instrument of our Latin American diplomacy.

Our sour beginnings in the Philippines are long since repaired. Pledges of independence were accepted; the visible symbols of schools and public improvements were proof of good faith. The Filipinos were faithful allies in the Second World War and, now an independent nation, they remain so.

But while the United States was able to turn the Philippines free, it cannot withdraw from the consequences of having entered them in the beginning. The game of "might have been" is fruitless, but it is likely that without the events of 1898 the United States and Japan might never have had the confrontation that led to Pearl Harbor.

America's involvement in Asia grows instead of shrinking, in labyrinthine ways that appear to have no exits. These, too, have their origins in a time when a war was splendid, when McKinley walked the floor in the White House and was told personally by God that he should annex the Philippines.

Mr. Andrist, an editor in the American Heritage Book Division, is the author of The Long Death: The Last Days of the Plains Indians *(Macmillan, 1964).*

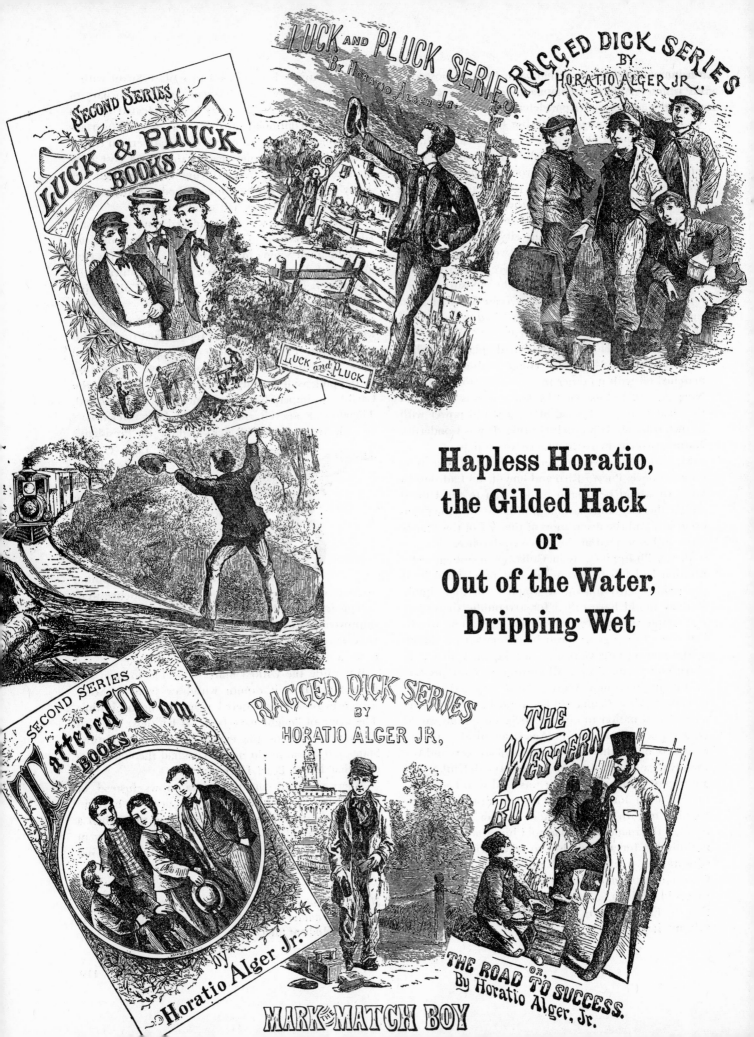

Hapless Horatio,
the Gilded Hack
or
Out of the Water,
Dripping Wet

"At the child's scream, the father looked up, and, with a cry of horror, sprang to the edge of the boat. He would have plunged in, but, being unable to swim, would only have endangered his own life, without being able to save his child. 'My child!' he exclaimed in anguish—'who will save my child? A thousand—ten thousand dollars to anyone who will save him!'"

Who indeed? The thousands of beardless readers of this soggy saga, first serialized in *Student and Schoolmate* during 1867, had no doubt who the rescuer would be; why else had the author positioned his young hero, Richard Hunter, on the fantail of the ferryboat at the beginning of Chapter XXVI? These readers would not be disappointed. Nor would the millions who would later pick their way through the contrived adventures of *Ragged Dick,* issued the following year in novel form, and the more than one hundred variations on the same formula-theme that Horatio Alger, Jr., produced before his death, at sixty-seven, in 1899.

In the end, Alger concluded—correctly—that he had been a failure, that he had wasted his life penning juvenile trash and carrying the bass drum in the band of the Newsboys' Lodging House atop the old *Sun* building in lower Manhattan. What probably disturbed him most was that he was the antithesis of his own characters. Poverty and hardship were the essential facts of their young lives, though they seemed always strong, stoutly built, and possessed of fresh complexions; their language was sharpened by the wit of the streets, where they were educated. Alger, however, was the son of a respectable Unitarian minister in Massachusetts, who put him through Harvard; he was pudgy, stoop-shouldered, bald, and as timid as his heroes were self-reliant; he stuttered. His heroes, for all their "Luck & Pluck," plied their trades diligently and conscientiously. Their author was as disorganized as the Mad Hatter, scattering his characters from volume to volume (he often had three or four under way at once), but productive: he cranked out a biography of the martyred James A. Garfield in thirteen days. And whereas his creations displayed an intuitive grasp for commercial affairs, Alger himself was a deplorable businessman, often selling his manuscripts outright, without regard for royalties. Characteristically, it never occurred to Alger that, in his depiction of the Victorian auctioneer raising the bidding on the life of his son, he had effectively skewered the value structure of the Gilded Age.

Meanwhile, "the ferry-boat was receding fast," but still Alger hesitated at the rail; the economic motivation of his own creation apparently proved too much for him, and he resolved to correct the impression, even as the victim went under for the second time: "[Ragged Dick's] determination was formed before he heard the liberal offer made by the boy's father." One senses the personal agony of this descendant of the Massachusetts Bay Colony as he sat, pen in hand, rereading his own sentence; no, something stronger was required: "Indeed," he continued, "I must do Dick the justice to say that, in the excitement of the moment, he did not hear it at all, nor would it have stimulated the alacrity with which he sprang to the rescue of the little boy."

Alas, Horatio, too late! You stand exposed. Human life, like everything else in the new urban-industrial world of the Nineties, has a price tag on it; the ferry does not stop because, in a mechanical society, the machine comes to the aid of man only if the schedule is not interrupted. What's worse, the father does not invoke God's name until *after* his son is saved, then proceeds to renege on his reward, offering Dick instead a tedious position in his counting-house. Commerce is in the saddle and rides mankind; hypocrisy has become a fact of life. Alger, himself an ordained minister, fails to remark upon the father's deceit; nor does the father offer any compensation for the two fishermen who, conveniently enough, rowed over and "seized Dick and his youthful burden, and drew them into the boat, both dripping with water."

No matter. The man who produced that sentence should not be questioned too closely about the flaws in his little economic sermonettes. The important thing now is Achievement: this was the altar Alger worshipped at so devoutly that, in Russel Crouse's phrase, he "even admired city aldermen." But in the process, Alger demonstrated how far this country had moved away from the rural democracy of Benjamin Franklin's America, which had been so deeply suspicious of the dehumanizing centralism of mercantilism. To the physiocratic Franklin, the only honest path to solvency was agricultural; the other sources of national wealth were war, which was robbery, and *"commerce, which is generally cheating."* The virtue of thrift may link these two periods, but to the colonial mind frugality was the basis of agrarian self-sufficiency; in the schemata of post-Civil War America, thrift led to investment and wealth, which in turn became power and success. And if this economic revolution was to succeed, thrift had to give way (and did) to credit, installment buying, and planned obsolescence. Inadvertently, then, Alger also holds up a mirror to the present. Ragged Dick—assuming he could obtain working papers, evade the truant officer, and locate an operating ferry— might think twice today about collecting any kind of reward and thus jeopardizing his family's Aid to Dependent Children payments. Unless, of course, the drowning child's father happens to be in a favorable capital-gains situation and is willing to make an annuity arrangement in oil stocks, with lucrative depletion allowances. Ah, but by this time, as a union official for the deck hands negotiates a hazardous-duty proviso in the contract to end the wildcat strike, the murky, polluted waters of the river have carried off their youthful burden.

By ROBERT S. GALLAGHER

Innocent Merriment

CONTINUED FROM PAGE 105

land sounds wonderfully exciting even now, and arc lights, though hard, shine with a splendid glitter.

Divorced not once but several times, the unforgettable Lillian Russell shone with the gemlike hardness of the stones Jim Brady gave her in such large numbers, and was, of all the stars, the one who most typified the era. She was born Helen Louise Leonard in Clinton, Iowa, but began reshaping reality in her very first job, appearing at Tony Pastor's variety theatre in 1880 as "Lillian Russell, the English Ballad Singer." She was then eighteen years old. Her father called her "airy, fairy Lillian"; a theatregoer overheard by a *Times* reporter called her "that delicious creature, the incarnation of peaches and cream"; and years later when she had retired into a society marriage, President Warren G. Harding called her Assistant Commissioner of Immigration. Even in that administration it was a breathtaking appointment. The great statesman sent her to Europe, remarking, "A woman's ear can get more information from Europeans than all the intelligence and diplomacy of the government." And what did Nestor-in-the-guise-of-Venus find out? She decided we were letting in too many foreigners.

Lillian achieved stardom, fittingly enough, just at the beginning of the Mauve Decade, when she appeared in the title role of Offenbach's *Grand Duchess.* Producer Rudolph Aronson spared no expense in making it a super-spectacle. It concerned itself with the Duchess of Gérolstein, who fell in love with Fritz, a recruit in her army, and made him a general. Meanwhile, however, Fritz had fallen in love with a peasant girl named Wanda, and when the Duchess discovered ... but then what did we say at the beginning of the article about what audiences wanted? The next year Lillian signalled the beginning of the mechanical riches of the coming century by singing into a metal horn in Chicago and being heard—courtesy of Mr. Bell—by President Cleveland in Washington.

By the time Miss Russell returned to Chicago for the Fair of 1893, she was earning something over two thousand dollars a week and was the undisputed queen of that perfectly Ninety-ish form, the operetta, a genre that in those days had all the cultural credit of real opera without the depressing prospect of anything disagreeable happening to the hero or heroine.

Attendance figures at the Fair bear out the notion of the nation's holiday mood. On May 1 the President pushed a button to turn on some of the new electric lights and open the exposition, and four days later the collapse of share prices for the National Cordage Company started what was to be a very copious bloodletting for the national economy. Some Americans were ruined, some were jobless, and some went hungry, but a startling number laughed at the slump, drew out their savings, and followed Jim Brady to Chicago. Railroad service had been getting better all the time (something perhaps hard to believe today), and going to Chicago was as easy as hitching up and going down to the depot. On October 9, when the recession was well established and giving no signs of easing, 761,942 people passed through the turnstiles in Chicago.

What did they see when they got inside? Educational things like the Fisheries Building, all covered with sculptured fish and lobsters, glamorous things like Lillian Russell singing "La Cigale" at the Midway Plaisance, daring things like the Levantine wiggling of Little Egypt (her memory kept the vogue of the Turkish Corner going in American homes for another ten years), and dramatic things like Belasco's production of *The Girl I Left Behind Me,* in which Apaches whooped in the wings getting ready to storm the fort, while the colonel's daughter comforted the wounded, prayed over the dead, and reminded her father to save a bullet for her.

If the Apaches in the wings weren't enough for you, you could go outside the fairgrounds and see Buffalo Bill's Wild West Congress of Rough Riders of the World, probably the most spectacular live show to be put on since the Romans flooded the Colosseum and staged a sea battle for the populace. Europe had already thrilled to Cody's extravaganza, so much so that several European countries had been persuaded to lend squads of regular cavalry troopers to add their rich regalia and rigid riding discipline to the show. The entire troupe numbered something more than a battalion, with 640 cowboys, Indians, soldiers, Arabs, Cossacks, ticket-takers, and others on the Cody payroll, and an advance guard of twelve press agents thundering the merits of the show. As for special effects—"God is my property man," said Buffalo Bill.

To audiences the show was the whole endless, agonizing winning of the West distilled into a pleasant, risk-free afternoon. No one was killed when the Indians pursued the old stagecoach around the ring—indeed it was customary to let celebrities ride in the coach, and John L. Sullivan reported it a bracing experience. The Pony Express riders, demonstrating the intricate art that had so quickly been rendered pointless by the railroad, never lost a letter to flood, fire, or arrow; and Annie Oakley, the prettied-up pioneer woman, demonstrated "dexterity of firearms."

Cody, who had played an active and genuine part in the history that shaped his show, sometimes found the grease paint a little thick. "As a fellow gets old," he told press agent Dexter Fellows, "he doesn't feel like tearing about the country forever. I do not want to die a showman. I grow very tired of this sort of sham worship sometimes." But this was not his only headache.

Not all the details of this enterprise could be left to God, and Cody soon discovered what many already knew, that big business is complicated, tiresome, and not something that one can take care of in his spare time. The new impresarios of the period were, in fact, more businessmen than showmen. The dedication of the Daly type of manager, who spent most of his time in an orchestra seat supervising a production, gave way to the calculations of a theatre syndicate, whose members spent most of their time over ledgers in New York while the shows they produced rode the rails.

No one knows who first had the idea, but the original group that met to form a national theatre syndicate consisted of Charles Frohman and Al Hayman of New York, as well as a pair of managers from Boston, a pair from Philadelphia, and the theatrical booking agents Marc Klaw and Abraham Erlanger. They could not possibly control all the road operations in a country in which almost every village of more than one thousand

This 1892 cartoon bemoans the taking over of the theatre by s-x, while the muse of drama, with broken lyre and tattered garb, is reduced to beggary. Plus ça change . . .

had some sort of covered space called an opera house, and that had, by 1900, over four hundred communities with populations of over five thousand, but the syndicate men used the prestige of New York productions and the ease of railroad transportation to bring more and more theatres under their control.

Some stars tried to fight for the right to control their own destinies; and the great Sarah Bernhardt played in circus tents and mouldy halls rather than accept dictation as to routes and plays. Richard Mansfield—perhaps not the greatest of actors, but the one American actor of the Nineties who consistently tried to raise the intellectual level of the theatre—fought the syndicate with no more success than he enjoyed when he tried to introduce Bernard Shaw to Broadway. On September 17, 1894, Mansfield produced *Arms and the Man* in New York to critical praise, and stubbornly kept it in his repertoire for several years, despite the fact that it never filled a house.

In October, 1897, Mansfield gave Shaw's *Devil's Disciple* its world premiere, remarking in a letter to a friend, "All fine and intelligent people are sure to like the play, for which reason we don't expect it to run." In his determination to do Shaw right, Mansfield even defied Shaw. The author had indicated that Dick Dudgeon's cousin Essie should be seventeen, in order to suggest a little shadowy romance in scenes between herself and Dudgeon. Mansfield sturdily cast the part as a waif of ten and replied to Shaw's cabled plea for "heart interest" with a forthright "heart interest be damned." Confused and flabbergasted by opposition, Shaw could think of nothing better to reply than "Same to you." To everyone's surprise, the play enjoyed a moderate success.

Mansfield's biggest hit, *Beau Brummell*, was written by Clyde Fitch, a man much more in tune with the times than Shaw. Fitch was a carpenter who shaped his graceful, well-joined little vehicles to the stars who would drive them. He was less successful when he tried to make the star fit his play; and Julia Marlowe objected to going gray between scenes over the death of her lover in *Barbara Frietchie* just so that Fitch could use the line " 'Who touches a hair of yon gray head, dies like a dog. March on,' he said."

Brummell, however, was just the kind of detached, bittersweet romance for the thoughtful Mansfield, as *Nathan Hale* and *The Cowboy and the Lady* were perfect for the tempestuous star team of Nat Goodwin and his third wife, Maxine Elliott. The difficult Goodwin, after an argument with Miss Elliott, once told his Lambs' Club cronies, "I thought I'd married the most beautiful woman in the world and I find my wife is a Roman senator."

Charles Hoyt, whose *A Trip to Chinatown* ran 650

ADDING INSULT TO INJURY.

Miss Hattie Gainsborough *(after the curtain went down)*. — Why, were you sitting right behind us all the afternoon, Mr. Short? How did you like the play?

performances in 1891–93, had tickets for the opening night of *Nathan Hale* and offered one to a friend, who replied forthrightly, "I wouldn't like it. I don't like Goodwin as a man. I don't like him as an actor."

"You'll like him in this play," said Hoyt. "They hang him in the last act."

The Cowboy and the Lady, with its confrontation of oversimplified eastern and western attitudes, was another hit, although London, unconcerned with American social patterns, found it a bore. American social patterns played little part in such hits of the Nineties as *Beau Brummell, The Prisoner of Zenda, Cyrano de Bergerac,* and *Trilby.* The only American pattern to be found in the sensationally successful *Sign of the Cross* was a Yankee desire for the best of both worlds, in this case, a leg show with a lesson. "Burleycue" was one thing, while Nero slavering over shrinking Christian slave girls in garments guaranteed not to choke his hungry lions was another. As morally acceptable as a lantern-slide trip to the Holy Land and somehow more gripping, *The Sign of the Cross* never aroused any of the protests that were likely to erupt about plays involving divorce or infidelity.

Some American playwrights were, however, beginning to try to write drama that was more profoundly native than was *The Cowboy and the Lady,* and perhaps the best of these writers was Augustus Thomas, whose series of state-named plays began in 1891 with *Alabama,* a rather sentimental effort about the Civil War, and then arrived at a new level two years later with *In Mizzoura,* whose sheriff hero, as played by Nat Goodwin, was something more than the laconic, legal gunman of other western plays.

Most of the time, though, great throbbing chords of hokum drowned out the plaintive pipe of theatrical progress, and the crowds that turned out to see Lillian Russell play twins in *Giroflé-Girofla,* or to marvel at the mechanical snowstorm in *Way Down East,* or to see DeWolf Hopper in jolly nonsense like *Wang, Wang Goes with a Bang,* and *Panjandrum* had no complaints against what the syndicate was giving them.

Indeed, in the case of Miss Russell, the public began to find her light operas not quite light enough, and the shrewd Lillian stopped in mid high C and went off to join Weber and Fields in their new Music Hall. Here she played parodies of the kind of thing she had done for real, making her debut in *Whirl-i-Gig,* a spoof of *The Girl from Maxim's,* at a gala opening for which the boxes were auctioned to such men about town as Stanford White, William Randolph Hearst, and the ever-faithful Jim Brady. Through all of Lillian Russell's marriages her friendship with Diamond Jim remained constant, and Jim, who like Louis XIV had both official and unofficial mistresses, offered Lillian his hand in marriage and filled the hand with negotiable bonds, the surest sign of sincerity he could conceive. She said No: she liked him too much to marry him.

This winning pair of contradictory people were, as much as two people can be, characteristic of the flamboyant age they dominated in so many ways. Their Nineties were indeed gay, although millions of Americans who were slaving away in factories, mines, and fields were unaware of that special quality in their era.

Still, when they turned out for the one day in the year when—according to the red-lined data in their Robert B. Mantell Pocket Calendars—the Robert B. Mantell theatrical troupe would be at their town's opera house, they touched the edge of the great gay carousel that circled the completed nation, and their children sometimes traded for a Lillian Russell cigarette card or saw Jim Brady's private car on a siding. Jim made his fortune by selling railroad supplies and got ahead of the competition by personally checking every mile of line from a handcar: the only handcar operator who ever wore a cutaway, a silk hat, and—still a beginner—only one or two small diamonds.

When we say "Gay Nineties" we often think of popping champagne corks and snapping garters—and indeed Koster and Bial's Cork Room Restaurant had over thirty thousand autographed corks around the walls, while establishments from Chicago's notorious "Slide" to discreet side-street "wine rooms" existed for the convenience of roués. Certainly Jim Brady knew a number of these addresses, and Stanford White gave him the first of the parties featuring nude girls jumping out of pies as a dessert course. But when Jim and Lillian really wanted to have fun, they went bicycling to a Jersey beer garden, an attendant pedalling behind with a jug of orange juice for teetotaller Brady.

The attendant also presided over the special electrobath where Jim's collection of cycles was periodically gold-plated, checked that none of the jewels set in the frames had worked loose, or, on occasion, did most of the pedalling on Jim's bicycle-built-for-three, while Jim, in a shepherd's plaid cycling outfit, and Lillian, in a white serge bloomer-suit, gossiped away up front.

Sometimes Jim and Lillian cycled in Central Park, she on the $1,900 cycle that Jim had given her and that travelled everywhere with her in a plush-lined case, and he on one of his assortment of rolling treasure chests. The crowds would grow to such proportions that Jim would have to distribute five-dollar bills among the bicycle-mounted police, who then would form a cordon around the royal riders. Another of their strange, innocent passions was the discovery of new ways to cook corn. Chicago millionaires, stroking their mustaches and gloating over a date with the Queen of the Fair, would be left at the stage door, the roses wilting in their hands, if Jim showed up with the address of a place that had a new butter sauce or a secret cream bath for the golden kernels. Off they would go, as rosily greedy as a pair of giant babies.

Jim always sat in the front row at Broadway openings and cried copiously at the calculated sentimentalities of melodrama. Sometimes, with the simple arrogance of a child, he addressed remarks to actor friends on stage. Sometimes, with the caution of those who depend on patronage, the actors replied.

Jim and Lillian and those they apotheosized were all relatively new at the game of seeking pleasure. In their favor one must say that they brought a vast zest to everything they did. One cannot, after all, imagine the society that Marcel Proust showed us getting all febrile about a corn roast. Against them one must mention that they insisted that every form of art turn its attention to entertainment, and that all the muses must sing for their suppers. It is characteristic that the most famous musical organization of the period was John Philip Sousa's band, which whammed out "Dixie" and excerpts from Sousa's comic opera *El Capitan,* when it wasn't doing Beethoven specially scored for brass.

The sugarplum songs of Victor Herbert, played by seedy trios masked by potted palms, gave rise to the comfortable definition "semiclassical" and convinced the people lunching at the better hotels that their taste was superior to that of the crowds listening to Maggie Cline, "the Irish Queen," singing "Throw Him Down, McCloskey," and "Down Went McGinty"; or to Ned Harrigan singing "Mrs. Murphy's Home" in his show *Reilly and the 400.* This last confection mocked the pompous Ward McAllister and his list of utterly "ins"

qualified to fill Mrs. Astor's 400-capacity ballroom. *Reilly and the 400* also gave America its first sweater girl in the person of Ada Lewis, who came on stage *without corsets* and made such a thing of a one-line part that Harrigan added to her role from night to night and finally launched her into a string of Tough-Girl-With-Heart-of-Gold characters.

Miss Cline's great number, "McCloskey," was one of the super-hits of the decade, and when she came to the title line, it was customary for everyone backstage to throw something, a stage brace, a chair, an iron bar, or whatever they could get their hands on, to the floor in a great whomping crash. The audience would reinforce the explosion with a roar of their own.

The best days of the minstrel shows lay behind the Gay Nineties as the American Negro began to make a place for himself in the entertainment world and to crowd out the burnt-cork brigade that had been giving a shadowy imitation of a plantation-porch daydream; and the best days of Chautauqua, that Lincoln Center under canvas, were to be in the first decade of the new century. It had been growing steadily since forty Sunday-school teachers in 1873 had paid six dollars each for two weeks of improving talks at a defunct campsite at Lake Chautauqua, and by 1900 there were two hundred establishments around the country. Still, the Nineties weren't all that strong on self-improvement, and the giant tents full of people listening to speakers were to be a phenomenon of the go-getter period of Babbitt rather than the good-time days of Brady.

The playgrounds in which these diamonds sparkled were as new as the settings of Jim's "transportation sets" of links and studs, in which the railroad-supply salesman celebrated every form of goods transportation ever known to man. In 1890 the Goelets opened the Imperial Hotel at Broadway and Thirty-second Street, and the smart world began to flock to its luxurious Palm Room. In a year they were calling for their Palm Room checks and hurrying up to the Holland House, built at a cost of more than a million dollars. The next year saw the completion of the Savoy, which had been started by Boss Tweed and finished by an investors' syndicate at a cost greater than even Tweed, builder of the world's most expensive courthouse, could imagine—or raise. The grandest caravansary, however, grew up as a result of an unseemly family quarrel. When the William Waldorf Astors were unable to wrest social leadership from his aunt, Mrs. William Backhouse Astor, he put up a big hotel (the Waldorf) next door to her home on Thirty-fourth Street, a front house, so to speak, that quite overshadowed the back house. Auntie huffed away to build a new pleasure dome farther uptown, and on the site of her old home appeared the Astoria. When peace was made in the family, the hotels were united, as in the ending of a good melodrama, and the Waldorf-Astoria became the newest and brightest stop on the round of gaiety. Theatres were popping open too, almost as fast as they are closing today.

In an age when the big openings are those of shopping centers, motels, and discotheques, one hesitates to call the Nineties frivolous. Two men of the period, David Belasco and William Gillette, were to go on and cut a considerable swath in the new century, Belasco because he was enough of an artist to be genuinely creative and enough of a businessman to stay alive while he did so, and Gillette because he foreshadowed a new school of acting, a new approach to the theatre. Gillette introduced to America the two-edged sword of naturalism.

His plays, which he wrote himself, had none of the genuine realism that Konstantin Stanislavski was finding in Chekhov, but the leading characters seemed always to stand out from the ranting supporting players and the lurid situations by the very quiet directness of their manner. The product of an old Connecticut family, Gillette attended both Harvard and Yale and got into the theatre with some help from Mark Twain, who managed to find him a bit in a touring company of *The Gilded Age.*

Gillette's acting was the kind that long afterward was to prove suitable to the movies, where the thoughts need not be projected but are picked off the face by the probing eye of the camera; and just about the time he was perfecting this art, the first movies were shown in America. Something moving on a screen appears to have been seen first in 1895 at the Cotton States Exposition in Atlanta, Georgia, and a year later ocean waves and other simple movements were visible to enthusiastic ticket-buyers at Koster and Bial's Music Hall. The first theatrical film was inspired by the Spanish-American War. In a small, well-lit room an actor, if that is the word, removed a Spanish flag from a small pole and trampled on it. Then he moved into the second, resolution act by running up an American flag instead.

Mechanical stunts in the theatre were growing more elaborate every season, and by 1899 the simple buzz-saw effect of *Blue Jeans* had given way to the chariot-race treadmill of *Ben Hur.* At Tattersall's in Chicago you could see a whole restaging of the sinking of the *Maine* and the Battle of Santiago done by miniature battleships that were just big enough to hold a human operator and a battery of controls for torpedoes and explosion effects. One imagines that the *Maine* was operated by remote control.

Things were getting bigger all the time. On New Year's Eve of 1900 there were five openings on Broad-

way, and although the titles, *The Burgomaster, In the Palace of the King, Sweet Nell of Old Drury, Mrs. Dane's Defense,* and *David Garrick,* do not suggest the theatre of Aristotle, they were certainly just the thing to precede a New Year's party (as for the theatre of Aristotle, Ibsen's *Master Builder,* which aspires to it, had managed only a single performance earlier in the same year). Later that season *The Floradora Girl* was the first big hit of the new century, and the pretty girls of the "Floradora Sextette" were the toast of thousands of college boys, hundreds of florists, and dozens of jewellers. It was the celebrity era.

Actors too wanted a share in the piles of money that seemed so ready for the taking in the booming entertainment business, and so lots of them became businessmen. "We all have bicycle faces," wrote E. H. Sothern in mourning the passing of Joseph Jefferson, a star of the golden age, "hard and set, tense and eager-looking. ... It has become necessary to assert oneself more and more or suffer the humiliation of being forced into the rear ranks." But when they became businessmen, they shared in the melon and bought great country houses and had a good time, which no one can begrudge them.

"As one who saw the syndicate rise and fall and fought it every step of the way," wrote William A. Brady in 1937, "I can tell you that its injection of big business into the theatrical game had more to do with the decline of the American theatre than any other ten things you can mention."

Ill health was a long time coming, however, and it must be said that the fun was considerable as the theatres shook to Maggie Cline's "McCloskey," vibrated to Lillian Russell's high C's, thrilled to Sherlock Holmes's outwitting of Professor Moriarty, hushed to the perfection of Ada Rehan, and pulsed with sentimental adoration of Maude Adams, while everyone loved hard-drinking Bill Cody, hard-punching John L. Sullivan, and hard-living Jim Brady, Master of the Revels of the Mauve Decade.

As a summing up, one thinks of the words of Lord Melbourne when the young Queen Victoria inveighed against the pleasure-seeking wickedness of her royal uncles and promised a reign of aspiration and progress. The old statesman listened to the admirable idealism of the young Queen, thought of the silly, wasteful parties, the staggerings home at late hours, the money lost in gambling sessions at clubs, the hangovers, and yet—and yet entered a small demurrer.

"But, Madame," he said, "they were such jolly men."

Mr. Broun, an actor for many years on Broadway and off, is the author of a recent book about the theatre entitled A Studied Madness. *He also covers special sporting events for the CBS television network.*

CONTINUED FROM PAGE 11

the government regulation they deplore in principle. To the Browns he is the great American villain, a living, breathing dollar sign, a corrupter of railroads and legislators, the murderer of free competition—the fellow who makes them pay double for their kerosene and axle grease.

Rockefeller deals in millions but watches the pennies. His order to use one less drop of solder in oil cans, for example, has effected a large long-term saving. He speaks so warmly of Standard's benevolence that the New York *Herald* remarks, "The only thing this company lacks is a . . . twenty-five-thousand-dollar chaplain who would open their meetings with religious services. . . ." Rockefeller is becoming so overburdened with money as to worry about getting rid of it. His solution is to set up a series of munificent public benefactions that will ultimately reach a colossal half billion, with the Reverend Frederick T. Gates as almoner. But in 1890 President Harrison signs the antitrust act named for Ohio's Senator John Sherman and passed almost unanimously by Congress. Rockefeller seemingly bows to the inevitable. He begins dismantling the trust he has erected, dividing it into twenty independent segments: "STANDARD GIANT TO SPLIT INTO MIDGETS," says a newspaper headline. In the end, however, the twenty companies are still controlled by Rockefeller, the monopoly remains intact, and other trusts are scarcely intimidated by the example. The Browns see no reduction in the price of petroleum products. The country is somewhat in the position of a patient who gets a prescription from a good physician and throws it away. Any really energetic prosecution of the Sherman Act will have to await the twentieth century and Theodore Roosevelt, now a talkative Civil Service commissioner.

Horse-trading in that same 1890 Congress results in the passage of two more bills that will have long reverberations. One is the measure calling for the government purchase of 4,500,000 ounces of silver monthly. The other is the highest tariff schedule yet devised—a bill framed by the handsome Representative William McKinley of Ohio.

The McKinley tariff mirrors the Republican faith in industrial prosperity and the perhaps less soulful belief that the protection of industry will spread benefits to the workers through higher wages. But retail prices advance immediately without any corresponding rise in wages. The new tariff receives a prompt rebuke at the polls. In the November congressional elections Republicans, including McKinley himself in Ohio, are turned out of office by the score. Out West the Browns have joined in a catchy new tune: *"I was a party man one time;/ The party would not mind me./ So now I'm working for myself,/ The party's left behind me."*

This is revolt. The extent of the revolt is indicated by the large number of "radicals" elected in the outland—among them William Jennings Bryan in Nebraska, Jerry Simpson in Kansas, and Ben Tillman as governor of South Carolina. The East's failure to understand agrarian problems is shown by its surprise at the election results, which *Harper's Weekly* calls "stunning." Few easterners notice the amazing feat of the unheard-of Bryan, an overpowering personality who can electrify audiences with a presence and a voice almost as big as the West itself. Bryan, campaigning in a district that had gone heavily Republican two years earlier, has won by a landslide.

Meanwhile the census is under way, causing some resentment because of the personal questions asked: Is your home mortgaged? Are you a pauper? Have you ever been convicted of a crime? Until 1880 the census, supervised by United States marshals who hired their own assistants, was notoriously unreliable. Now in 1890 it is pushed by enumerators working under a superintendent in Washington, and for the first time it makes use of punch cards and computing ma-

Everything was up to date in San Francisco. For an evening reserved seat of twenty-five cents you got a feast of goodies ranging from the latest flicks of Edison to burlesque. Along the way came a Wagnerian soprano from Dresden and "miramba" players from Guatemala. What Papinta's "new electrical effects" were, the poster prudently didn't say. That was what you paid your quarter for.

Sears, Roebuck sold this talking machine, complete with "new aluminum tone arm," for $45.

Rising skirts revealed more boot but no flesh.

chines, insuring greater accuracy as well as permitting the tabulation of broad data that will teach the nation much about itself. The enumerator calling on the Joneses is a well-brushed clerk responsible for only a few city blocks. The one visiting the Browns is a tobacco-chewing horseman who covers many miles.

The United States now has close to 63,000,000 people against the 50,000,000 of 1880, almost 5,000,000 of these new citizens being immigrants, the biggest influx in history. The new wave is so heavy with Italians and Russian Jews as to arouse anxiety among America's older families, who, of course, are predominantly of Anglo-Saxon origin. Many of the newcomers arrive in Dollar Land with empty pockets but hearts full of hope. Castle Garden is swamped with them, and by the end of the year Ellis Island will be opened to receive the incoming hordes, who so augment the labor force that union leaders complain that they cheapen labor and are often used as strikebreakers. Throngs of the Slavs move on to Pennsylvania and Ohio to work in the steel mills and mines, but most of the Italians remain in the big eastern cities. New York-Brooklyn has become the world's greatest melting pot, with half as many Italians as Naples, twice as many Irish as Dublin, as many Germans as Hamburg, and two and a half times as many Jews as Warsaw. Some immigrant children never see the inside of a schoolhouse. Water taps are scarce, saloons plentiful, boys become hardened drinkers at fourteen; winsome little girls become dollar-a-week clerks, and some inevitably swell the city's estimated total of 25,000 prostitutes. By 1890 there are some 35,000 New York tenements inhabited by over a million people, many past all hope.

The concept of social responsibility is still checked by the powerful tradition of individualism. Tammany pays these people enough spurious attention to win their votes. The "better classes," insulated from the poor and not without a nativist disdain, are largely indifferent until they are shocked by Jacob Riis's *How the Other Half Lives*, published in 1890. Riis, himself an immigrant from Denmark who has patrolled the slums as a newspaperman, tells Fifth Avenue all about Bottle Alley. One can imagine Mrs. Jones, horror-stricken, saying to her husband, "Can people be living like this only ten minutes away from us?"

Riis's book and his lectures spur a movement for reform that will make progress even if it will never quite catch up. In Chicago, Jane Addams' work at Hull House further heralds the waning of every-man-for-himself. In the South, Booker T. Washington has an even more formidable task in his efforts to elevate the biggest underprivileged minority, America's 7,000,000 Negroes.

Meanwhile the westward movement continues, and in 1889–90 North and South Dakota, Washington, Idaho, Montana, and Wyoming are admitted to statehood, putting forty-four stars on the flag. Utah is sternly forbidden entrance until it purges itself of the Mormon doctrine of polygamy. Wyoming becomes the first state to permit women to vote—only one of many signs of the changing West.

Another sign is apparent to the Browns in Kansas: they see as many giraffes as they do buffalo—that is, none of either. In 1869 a Kansas Pacific train had to wait from 9 A.M. to 5 P.M. for a vast herd of buffalo to cross the track. The K.P. no longer suffers such delays, for about 31,000,000 bison have been killed in a thirteen-year span, many of them shot by marksmen from trains by way of target practice. Now a Kansas rancher named C. J. Jones, realizing that they are almost extinct, searches for weeks to round up a small herd, some of which he sells to parks and zoos so that the great beast of the plains may not be forgotten.

Mining is booming in the West, but the prospector and sourdough have all but vanished and the mines are owned by capitalists. Homesteaders invade the once open and free grazing grounds and fences go up, spelling doom to the cattleman of the untrammelled herds and finishing off the Long Drive from Texas to Kansas. Cattle raising continues on a new basis, with more and smaller herds on fenced and privately owned land. The romantic, hell-for-leather cowboy of legend is gone except in the dime novels, having become a twenty-five-dollar-a-month hired hand reduced to mending fences. Even of these hands only some 15,000 remain, and an English socialist, Edward Aveling, visiting in America, urges them to join the Knights of Labor to better their condition. Nothing dramatizes the passing of the Old West more vividly than the fact that two-gun heroes such as Buffalo Bill Cody and Wild Bill Hickok have quit the West and are putting on whooping melodramas for city slickers.

Top-grade overstuffed couches for overstuffed parlors sold for $148.

The most pathetic of American minorities are the Indians, 250,000 of them, who for decades have been dispossessed, uprooted, mistreated, and swindled. Now another Sioux reservation in South Dakota is opened for homesteaders, the Indians being compensated with $1.25 an acre. But as with all such arrangements, they do not like it and submit only because there is no alternative. On December 15, 1890, the well-remembered Sitting Bull (who for a time was a headliner with Buffalo Bill's Wild West Show) is shot dead when soldiers try to arrest him on suspicion of fomenting trouble. On December 29, some 400 hungry Sioux under Chief Big Foot are intercepted by the 7th Cavalry, Custer's old command, near Wounded Knee Creek. Although Big Foot surrenders peacefully, a few of his braves rebel. The 500 well-armed troopers let loose with rifles and Hotchkiss machine guns, and Wounded Knee becomes a massacre as the Indians flee; many of the wounded freeze to death in a blizzard the next day. Nearly 300 of the Sioux, a majority of them women and children, are lost in this last important Army-Indian battle, one that will leave the redmen bitter for generations.

So the year 1890 ends on an unworthy note, with a lesson not lost on the growing number of libertarians—the lesson that one peril in a great democracy is to ignore minorities that have no political influence. The fact that two large volunteer organizations of white men are working energetically to improve the Indians' lot is far more typical than the sad error in South Dakota. If the whole nation resembles an Englishman's description of New York—"a lady in ball costume, with diamonds in her ears, and her boots out at the toes"—the lady is finally giving thought to her boots. The public social conscience is not yet big but it is growing. There are strong movements against child labor, against sweatshops and slums; more support for broader education, for the eight-hour workday and the Saturday half-holiday; more good people who devote themselves to the betterment of others; more politicians who see that change is needed.

In 1898 Mother's wood-burning helper stood at five feet ten inches, cost about $100.

The prevailing mood is one of energy and confidence, a sublime certainty that problems can be solved, that this is the best country in the universe. There is no suspicion that the nation will soon face its worst panic and its most disastrous labor uprising almost simultaneously with the achievement of its grandest world's fair. The confidence is so pervasive that even farmers ruined in the West are able to joke wryly about it, heading eastward to make a new start with signs on their wagons, "In God we trusted, in Kansas we busted." But they are not so confoundedly joyful as to forget that they and the working men are the have-nots, and it is always the have-nots who first see the need for reform.

There lies the threat and also the promise of the years immediately ahead. The wonderful thing about America as it pushes into the Nineties is that it complains and quarrels and occasionally even curses, but still its vast majority is guided by bright hope and the intention to make things right by orderly political action. The United States is one of the very few places in the world where such a thing is possible.

The Joneses on their bicycles and the Browns in their rumbling plank wagon are rolling faster than they think into a tumultuous and unforgettable decade.

This eight-day clock sold for $7.20; with an alarm, 60¢ extra.

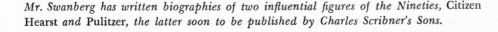

Mr. Swanberg has written biographies of two influential figures of the Nineties, Citizen Hearst *and* Pulitzer, *the latter soon to be published by Charles Scribner's Sons.*

tash; for dessert he fed his sweet tooth. He was a modest drinker, choosing Vichy water if he had a choice, but a fierce smoker of Havana cigars. Hanna rarely read a book except, out of family pride, the histories of James Ford Rhodes, his eminent and brilliant brother-in-law. His love was the theatre, and as a rich man he indulged himself by owning one. He liked to be in the company of actors. Touring players found generous hospitality at Hanna's home. The son of a Quaker and a Presbyterian, the husband of an Episcopalian, Hanna kept his own religion secret, if he had any. The only way he'd get to heaven, he once said, would be on his wife's coattails.

He was a family man, father of a son and two daughters. (One of the girls, Ruth, was to serve in Congress.) His wife, Charlotte Augusta Hanna, known as "Gussie," was tall, reserved, and charming and had been to a New York finishing school. At least one observer saw in the union of roughshod Mark Hanna and cultivated Charlotte Rhodes "a quality of pure romance."

Mark Hanna was born on September 24, 1837, in New Lisbon, a small town on the eastern border of Ohio, where the merchant Hannas were considered very prominent people until they lost $200,000 in a canal venture. Then they moved to Cleveland and became wholesale grocers. Mark briefly attended Western Reserve College, but when his father died, at the beginning of the Civil War, it became his responsibility to represent his mother in the family business. So in the fashion of the time he hired a substitute to fight for him, although as a National Guard lieutenant he served a bloodless hundred days. In 1864 he married the daughter of Daniel Rhodes, an imperious coal and iron merchant.

It was on the foundation of his father-in-law's business that Hanna built an industrial empire. M. A. Hanna & Company, successor to Rhodes & Company, grew horizontally—from selling to transporting to owning the ships to building them to mining to manufacturing. Hanna's business was personal—a partnership, not a corporation; built through reinvestment rather than with outside capital. It was always essentially local, in character and scope a Great Lakes concern.

The most remarkable aspect of Hanna the businessman was his advanced views on organized labor. In 1876 the secretary of the Miners' National Association testified: "He was the first mining operator in the bi-tuminous fields of the United States to recognize the cardinal principle of arbitration in the settlement of wage disputes, and the first also to recognize the Miners' National Association." Hanna was enraged when George Pullman refused to arbitrate the great railroad strike of 1894. "A man who won't meet his men half-way is a God-damn fool!" Hanna shouted at his fellow members of the Cleveland Union Club. Myron Herrick, the banker, tried to quiet him; he was making a scene. Another friend wished Hanna to remember that the town of Pullman provided neat homes for workers. "Oh, hell!" snorted Hanna. "Go and live in Pullman and find out how much Pullman gets sellin' city water and gas ten per cent higher to those poor fools!" (Hanna's words spread to Chicago, and in 1896 he had trouble getting a campaign contribution from the Pullman Company.)

Murat Halstead, the Cincinnati editor, explained to the readers of the *Review of Reviews* in October, 1896: "It is a blunder on the part of those who assail Mr. Hanna to hold that he is exclusively or exceptionally a man of dollars. He has had enough of them long enough to know the weakness as well as the power of money." As Hanna grew bored with the business of business in the 1880's, he began dabbling in politics. At first he was merely another rich contributor and collector of campaign funds, and in 1891 he was asked to become treasurer of the Republican National Committee. But Hanna declined; he had other ideas of his future political role.

From the very beginning Hanna saw himself as the manager; elective or appointive office never tempted him. As early as 1885 he declined an honorary position with the governor's militia that carried the mouth-watering title of general. General Hanna. It interested him not at all. He was a king-maker in search of a king. He was also a hero-worshipper in search of a hero.

But settling on a hero-king in Ohio politics was a tricky business. "No Republican politician in Ohio trusts any other Republican politician," wrote the *Nation,* "and all of them expect 'treachery' as a matter of course." In Ohio, politics was everybody's second job, and every year was an election year. Before he chose William McKinley, Hanna had two trial runs.

His first choice was John T. Sherman, younger brother of the illustrious Civil War general, who had served continuously in House, Senate, or Cabinet since 1855. Known in Ohio as "the Mansfield icicle," he was capable and cool, with an immense capacity for being dignified, which was confidence-inspiring if not inspirational. In 1884 and again in 1888, Hanna was pledged to make him President, in the latter year serving as his manager. But when Blaine and then Harrison were preferred over Sherman, it was clear that "Uncle Jawn" was strictly a loser. And the one thing an aspiring political manager cannot afford is to back a loser.

Between the 1884 and 1888 conventions, Hanna's second choice was Joseph Benson Foraker, who was about the same age as McKinley—both were in their early forties—and thus destined to be his rival. Of the two, Foraker was the more commanding personality, the better orator, the brighter man. More important to Hanna, however, Foraker was not lovable like McKinley. Foraker might have been President (he became governor of Ohio before McKinley), but he was a flawed politician—a loner, less loyal to party and persons than the standard required, and too transparently ambitious. At the 1888 convention, where Hanna was laboring so valiantly in the hopeless cause of Sherman, Foraker hinted broadly that the Ohio delegation would be wise to switch to a winner; McKinley, on the other hand, announced firmly that he would go down with the ship. It was over loyalty that Hanna and Foraker parted. "It was at this convention that I gained an insight into the unselfish, unfaltering loyalty which William McKinley gave to every cause he espoused," Hanna later told the editor of *National Magazine*. "And here for the first time, it occurred to me that he was a logical candidate for the Presidency in years to come."

They made a strange pair. From almost any angle—as speakers or listeners or dressers or money-makers—they were opposites. McKinley knew all the little subterfuges of being a public man; Hanna knew none. McKinley could shake thousands of hands without noticeable fatigue (he always firmly grasped the other fellow's hand first); Hanna's hand would swell painfully after a bout of handshaking. But together, as many analysts have noted, they made one perfect politician—although the mix was at least sixty per cent McKinley and forty per cent Hanna. It was not just that McKinley's presence, innate courtesy, and warmth made him the front man of the team. He also, in Joe Cannon's words, kept his ear so close to the ground that he got it full of grasshoppers. McKinley's grasshopper ear—his ability to take correct soundings on what his countrymen felt and wanted—made him a skillful practitioner of the art of the possible.

But the candidate lacked organizational talent, and here Hanna was a genius. After McKinley decided on the objectives, Hanna took over. His was the task of tactics and execution. Some, such as Republican National Committeeman Henry Clay Hansbrough of North Dakota, contended that "McKinley's nomination was a foregone conclusion even before Hanna began his fight for him." This may be true, but Hanna made it easy—and in so doing changed the contours of American politics.

Before Hanna, the political map was divided into state, or sometimes regional, fiefdoms, each led by a man like Platt, Quay, Powell Clayton of Arkansas, Henry C. Payne of Wisconsin. Never questioning the assumption that the nation was too vast to be manipulated by any one man, a candidate worked almost exclusively through these local factotums, only occasionally sending a missionary or two of his own into the field. Hanna, the political novice, spun his web over the whole country; campaigning on the slogan "The People Against the Bosses," he became the first national boss in modern American history.

A small cadre of workers operated under Hanna's command. From his Cleveland office in the Perry-Payne building on lower Superior Street, Hanna had direct telephone lines strung to the candidate's home in Canton, sixty-five miles away, where a young ex-reporter named Joseph P. Smith was the top staff man; to the Akron home of former state chairman Charles Dick; and later to Dawes in Chicago and to Will Osborne in New York. Osborne was not an especially astute politician; he had been best man at McKinley's wedding, and his chief quality was an unswerving loyalty to the candidate. Dick, on the other hand, was the man on whom Hanna relied to keep the machine well oiled. He was a superb handler of details, keeper of the index cards, compiler of all that had to be known on workers and precincts. Hanna's system of management worked in much the same manner as he answered his mail. Although at one time he averaged between six hundred and seven hundred letters daily, he wrote few in his own hand and did not have the ability to dictate. So in a few words he told his secretaries what he wished to say and left it to them to fill in the courtesies.

All this was done with so little personal fanfare that many at the St. Louis convention did not know how to spell "Hanna"; often a final "h" was added. Fewer still recognized the face when he rose to accept the applause of the delegates. But before the year was out his features would be familiar to every newspaper reader.

In a sense, it was Hanna's misfortune that his candidate was so "typically American." When *Judge* asked, "Are there two better American faces than those of McKinley and his charming wife?" the question was clearly rhetorical. (That poor Ida McKinley spent her adult life teetering on the brink of insanity apparently did not detract from her typicality; at the same time, it measurably contributed to the image of her devoted husband as a Christian martyr.) For those who wished to defeat the Republicans it was much simpler to attack Hanna.

William Randolph Hearst wished to defeat the Republicans. A millionaire by inheritance, a Democrat by conviction, and a publishing genius by instinct, he had moved to New York late in 1895 to try to pump life into the moribund *Journal*. It suited his politics and his drive for circulation to turn Mark Hanna into a bloated behemoth of plutocratic power. This job he entrusted to two men, Homer Davenport, a country-boy cartoonist who meant no harm when his powerful strokes besotted Hanna's features and turned him into a sordid monster in a dollar-sign suit; and political writer Alfred Henry Lewis, a reformed drunkard who meant as much harm as his vitriolic pen was capable of. Lewis described Hanna as "lacking utterly in human sympathy, a king of selfish egotism . . . cruel. What others suffer is of slight weight with him . . . loves money. Not for its yellow sake as a miser might, but for the sway and power thereof; because he may make men creep and crawl and spring to do his work . . . vain with all of the vulgarity and ostentatious strut of a turkey cock—a fowl, by the way, he much resembles . . . a tyrant. . . . What is weak he crushes from the merest instinct of destruction."

Hanna had other enemies. In Columbus, Ohio, anti-Hanna lyrics were written to the tune of "Just Before the Battle, Mother." In Pueblo, Colorado, the *Silver Party Song Book* instructed the faithful in "Hanner's Lullaby to the McKinley Kids":

> *Your Hanner will hold you*
> *And sing you to rest,*
> *As a fond lion foldeth*
> *The lambs to his breast.*
> *Hush, hush, hush-a-bye.*

And there were those who wished—quite unfairly—to paint Hanna as the Union Crusher, Relentless Foe of Organized Labor, Strikebreaker. In a Populist novel, *Waiting for the Signal,* this passage appeared:

Crash! Crash! Ping!—A flash of flame from a hundred rifle barrels, and Mark Hanna's ruffians came charging down the dock. At the first fire, John Stearns [worker-hero] threw up his hands and fell face downward. . . .

As the Pinkertons dashed over the prostrate forms of the slaughtered men, those in the rear hastily placed old revolvers and knives in the stiffening fingers of the corpses—an old trick practiced by detectives and deputies to deceive the people.

The target of these attacks was by no means thin-skinned; still, he resented them deeply and they poisoned his relations with the press for the rest of his life. During the 1896 campaign he showed Senator

Harper's Weekly, JUNE 27, 1896

In June the GOP convention at St. Louis nominated McKinley.

Nathan Bay Scott of West Virginia a Davenport cartoon and said: "That hurts . . . to be held up to the gaze of the world as a murderer of women and children, I tell you it hurts." Tears ran down his cheeks, and he turned and silently walked away.

If the Republican nomination in St. Louis was predictable, the Democratic nomination in Chicago was incredible, at least until, as William Jennings Bryan said, one examined "the logic of the situation." Grover Cleveland had been unlucky enough to be President during the Panic of 1893 and the ensuing depression in which as much as twenty per cent of the labor force was unemployed. Senator John Tyler Morgan of Alabama spoke for the South: "I hate the ground the man walks on." A weathered ex-congressman from Missouri, Richard P. Bland, was the leading candidate; but then, on July 8, the second day of the convention, a thirty-six-year-old delegate from Nebraska wearing a black alpaca coat strode to the platform. Forty minutes later, William Jennings Bryan reached the well-rehearsed peroration that would make him the Democratic presidential nominee—"You shall not press down upon the brow of labor this crown of thorns, you shall not crucify mankind upon a cross of gold." The issue—free and unlimited coinage of silver at a ratio of sixteen to one—had already captured the party; now it found its candidate.

"Free silver" may have smacked of quackery, but the forces behind it were starkly real. All those who needed inflation and cheap money—the debtors, the poor, the struggling farmers of the South and West—saw silver as their savior, and Bryan's description of the gold standard as a crucifixion of the have-nots roused them to an almost religious fervor.

Republican Chairman Hanna cancelled his plans to go yachting along the New England coast. He had expected an easy race against Bland; but now, he remarked, "The Chicago convention has changed everything."

McKinley still thought he could run on the tariff. "This money matter is unduly prominent," he told William R. Day, his former law partner. "In thirty days you won't hear anything about it." Day replied: "In my opinion in thirty days you won't hear of anything else."

Bryan quickly turned Day into a prophet. The nation had never known a campaigner remotely like him. Instead of staying home, as decorous candidates for the Presidency had always done, he packed his bag and set out to spread the free-silver gospel. At first he travelled alone on regular trains, often carrying his own luggage, sometimes walking from station to hotel. His itinerary was flexible to the point of whimsey. Not until October 7 did the Democratic National Committee provide him with a private railroad car, misnamed "The Idler." But his audiences were huge, and with the exception

In Chicago the next month, the Democrats named Bryan.

of some Yale students in New Haven, well behaved and enthusiastic. Seventy thousand listened on the Boston Common; even more turned out at Indianapolis, where Bryan rode in a white carriage drawn by four white horses in silver harness. He averaged sixty thousand to one hundred thousand words daily; on some days he gave twenty-seven speeches. The crowd in Aberdeen, South Dakota, waited six and a half hours to hear him. When the campaign was over, Bryan figured he had travelled 18,000 miles and delivered some six hundred speeches to perhaps five million people in twenty-seven states.

Hanna was worried. The early polls showed Bryan would carry Iowa. He felt McKinley should get "on the road to meet this thing." McKinley's reply was that a speech-making tour would be interpreted as a sign of weakness. "Moreover, I might just as well put up a trapeze on my front lawn and compete with some professional athlete as go out speaking against Bryan. I have to *think* when I speak."

If McKinley would not go to the people, Hanna would bring the people to McKinley. Forty-five minutes after his nomination the first delegation of two thousand arrived in Canton, coming the twenty miles from Alliance by a special train of the Pittsburgh, Fort Wayne and Chicago Railroad. It was followed by trains of the Interurban Electric; the Cleveland, Terminal and Valley; the Cleveland, Canton and Southern. They came from Massillon, Akron, Carrollton, Osnaburg, Minerva, Niles. "Rah, Rah, Right." "Who's all right?" "McKinley's all right." "Where was he born?" "N-I-L-E-S." In all, fifty thousand came on the day the little Major was made the Republican standard-bearer.

And they came day after day after day, through the summer heat and the fall rain, the people and the placards and the music: the Colored Republican League of New York, the Little Six Band of Upper Sandusky, the Old Tippecanoe Club of Chicago, the Foraker Club of Zanesville, the M. A. Hanna Club of Benwood, the McKinley and Hobart Club of Knoxville, the Frelinghuysen Escort Club of Newark, the Garfield Club of Louisville. Several thousand uniformed bicyclists from a dozen states had planned a program of intricate formations in front of the McKinley homestead but found the crowd too thick to permit them to perform. Eight hundred members of the Window Glass Workers of North America came to cheer the candidate; three thousand employees of the Carnegie Steel Works at Homestead appeared, waving signs reading, "Open the Mills—Shut the Mints." There were delegations of Hungarian-Americans, Italian-Americans, Polish-Americans. Two hundred women from Oil City, Pennsylvania, dressed in costumes to represent the forty-five states, were followed by three hundred men carrying red, white, and blue umbrellas. Students came from Allegheny College, the University of Chicago, Ohio State, Ohio Medical College. There were Buffalo lumbermen, and six hundred farmers. The "Heavy Weight McKinley Club" weighed in—"40,000 Pounds for McKinley—Not One Ounce for Bryan"; fifty stenographers; the Cadiz City Band; three hundred fifty employees of Hanna's Cleveland City Railway Co. ("prettily uniformed and unusually well drilled"); three hundred Lehigh Valley miners; two thousand former Confederate soldiers from Virginia giving the Rebel yell; the Grand Army Club of Maryland, the Allegheny Bar Association, the First Voters McKinley Drum Corps, the Ladies Marching Club of Cleveland. Some came because their employers wanted them to; most came because they wanted to.

They sang from before sunup till late at night, adjusting their words to everything from Negro spirituals to the latest popular hits: to the tunes of "Marching Through Georgia," "The Sunshine of Paradise Alley," "After the Ball," "Say Au Revoir but Not Goodbye," "The Band Played On," "Yankee Doodle," "Massa's in de Cold, Cold Ground," "Take Your Time, Miss Lucy," "Tramp, Tramp, Tramp," "John Brown's Body." One parody ran:

> McKinley, 'tis of thee,
> Great friend of liberty,
> Of thee we sing!

And they brought gifts for the candidate: watermelons, cheeses, glass canes, flags, flowers (real and artificial), cakes, clothing, five live American eagles, a marble bust of McKinley, a polished tree stump from Tennessee, a miniature gold reproduction of a steel rail, a sixty-foot sheet of tin, the largest plate of galvanized iron ever rolled in the United States. And they took home souvenirs: bits of the front porch; slivers from the McKinleys' picket fence; grapes from the McKinleys' arbor until there was no arbor; branches, twigs, leaves, shrubs, blades of grass. The McKinley lawn turned into a lake of mud. And still they came, especially on Saturdays, 750,000 of them in over three hundred delegations from thirty states.

A "Home Guard" of Canton men met the incoming trains, lined up the debarking delegations, marched them to North Market Street for the official McKinley greeting, sold them mementos of their visit, and got them back on their trains in time to greet the next arriving party. The candidate himself made sure that there would be no *faux pas* from an overzealous delegation chairman. As Charles Dick recalled:

... a letter would be sent to the national committee or to Canton saying that a delegation of farmers, cigarmakers, merchants or churchmen would call on McKinley on such

a day if agreeable. A letter would be written back asking that the man who would present the delegation be sent to Canton.

When the man appeared, McKinley would shake hands with him and ask: "You are going to present the delegation and make some remarks. What are you going to say?"

The man would reply: "Oh, I don't know; anything that occurs to me."

Then McKinley would say: "That will hardly do. Write out what you are going to say and let me see it a week or ten days ahead.... With your permission I shall make some suggestions and return it to you."

I know a man who went to Canton with his speech written out as requested by McKinley. "Just read it to me," McKinley said.

After he had finished, McKinley said: "My friend, that is a splendid speech, a magnificent speech; no one could have gotten up a better one, but this is not quite the occasion for such a speech.... It is sound and sober from your standpoint, but I have to look at it from the party's standpoint. Now, you go back home and write a speech along such and such lines and bring me a copy of it." The man came back with his new speech and McKinley blue-pencilled it until it suited him.

Therefore, when the leader of the delegation made his speech, McKinley knew days before what the orator would say and also what he would say in reply. Now that was politics.

The front porch campaign was political orthodoxy. Unlike his peripatetic opponent, McKinley was breaking no new ground, but never before had the old method been so mechanized, made so efficient, exploited so fully.

While Bryan was converting and McKinley was reassuring, Hanna was organizing. On the morning of July 28 the Republican chairman arrived in New York to start collecting his campaign kitty. He was discouraged to find important doors closed to him. Hanna's fortune was in Great Lakes millions; his reputation had not preceded him east. Back in Chicago, Dawes wrote in his diary, "August 24. Received letter from Hanna. The outlook for money ... is very poor. Our plans will have to be cut down." Part of Hanna's problem may have been, as John Hay wrote Henry Adams, that "[Bryan] has succeeded in scaring the Goldbugs out of their five wits; if he had scared them a little, they would have come down handsome to Hanna. But he has scared them so blue that they think they had better keep what they have got left in their pockets against the evil day."

Then Hanna had a stroke of good luck. Quite by accident he bumped into his old friend James J. Hill of the Great Northern, who, upon hearing Hanna's sad tale, took him on a five-day guided tour of Wall Street. Once Hanna's foot was squarely in the door, he made sure that he would never have to play beggar again. He levied regular assessments on the financial community—in the case of the banks it was one quarter of one per cent of their capital. Standard Oil made the largest contribution, $250,000. The great Chicago meat-packing firms reportedly gave a combined gift of $400,000. New York Life came through with $50,000, as did Equitable Life. Another $50,000 was given by the Milwaukee Road; the Illinois Central Railroad gave $35,000, plus an additional $20,000 from its president, Stuyvesant Fish; E. H. Harriman of Union Pacific kicked in $35,000; John W. ("Bet-you-a-million") Gates, $12,500; Marshall Field, $4,000. Prominent Democratic businessmen contributed handsomely, agreeing with the remark of New York's Senator David Hill, "I am still a Democrat—very still." Even in poor Vermont, where only $4,000 had been raised in 1892, Senator Justin Morrill now reported that he had collected $15,000. General Horace Porter set up a special committee to canvass for smaller checks, but in the GOP's Chicago office seventy-seven per cent of the reported contributions consisted of $1,000 or more. The Republican National Committee had a guarantee fund that was not called upon, for, as Charles Dick said, Hanna was offered more money than he could use.

The Democrats were having much more difficulty in raising money for Bryan. Senator Gorman of Maryland pleaded with Marcus Daly, owner of the fabulous Anaconda mines, for $350,000—"If it could be furnished within ten days," he wrote on September 29, "I am confident Bryan can win. You and you alone can have this amount raised—Can you? Will you do it?" Daly was generous; all told, he is said to have given $159,000 to Bryan's cause. But there were relatively few such "fat cats." Hearst ran a newspaper campaign that brought in $25,000, and added another $15,000 of his own money.

Yet the election would not be settled by cash. Even the hard-pressed Democrats probably had enough to tell their story adequately; moreover, their grand strategy, with its emphasis on the handsome young candidate, his fervor, his voice, and his boundless energy, was as economical as it was correct. And it suited Bryan's design to play the "poor boy." As McKinley said when discussing his reasons for not leaving Canton: "If I took a whole train, Bryan would take a sleeper; if I took a sleeper, Bryan would take a chair car; if I took a chair car, he would ride a freight train. I can't outdo him [in pleading poverty], and I am not going to try."

Each side conceded one third of the vote. The Republicans expected to lose most of the West and all of the South; the Democrats, despite a monster rally in Madison Square Garden, wrote off the East. The battleground would be the Middle West. Of Bryan's 249 major whistlestops, 160 would be in the nation's midsection.

The Republican campaign was to be directed at the laboring classes. As Will Osborne wrote to his candidate-cousin, "The people who have got property are all right and can take care of themselves." Labor had to be persuaded that any threat to the gold standard was a threat to their jobs. This would take, in the words of Hanna, a "campaign of education." He put William N. Hahn, a former Ohio GOP chairman, in charge of the speakers' bureau, with the responsibility for recruiting, training, directing, and scheduling 1,400

Harper's Weekly, MARCH 28, 1896

Before the convention, McKinley tried to keep quiet on the monetary issue. W. A. Rogers drew this lampoon, which he called "A Giant Straddle." Tom Reed of Maine, a rival for the nomination, put it this way: "McKinley does not want to be called a goldbug or a silverbug, so he has compromised on a straddlebug."

IN 1861
WILLIAM McKINLEY
WAS UPHOLDING HIS
COUNTRY'S HONOR,—

AND HE'S DOING
IT YET!

IN 1861
THIS IS WHAT
WILLIAM J. BRYAN
WAS DOING,—

AND HE'S DOING
IT YET!

Harper's Weekly, *firmly in McKinley's camp, went way back to the Civil War to discredit Bryan, who was born in 1860.*

speakers. About a third were paid professionals; the rest were volunteers who received only their expense money. Stump-speakers were specialists. Some talked only to foreign-language groups; several applicants with recommendations from Theodore Roosevelt and Republican Treasurer Cornelius Bliss were rejected because they didn't possess the right accents to address farmers. An estimated 16,500 Republican meetings were held in Ohio alone.

Then there were the "big guns"—Foraker spoke forty-six times in six days and gave almost two hundred speeches by election day; former President Harrison, after much grousing, finally agreed to give the "keynote address" at the Music Hall in New York City on August 28 and went on to make nearly fifty speeches by the end of the campaign; Terence V. Powderly, former grand master of the Knights of Labor, toured the industrial centers, and McKinley asked Chauncey M. Depew of the New York Central to tour the farm states. Depew replied, "Mr. McKinley, my position as a railroad president, I am afraid, would antagonize them." To which the Major answered, "On the contrary, your very position will draw the largest audience and receive the greater attention." Later, when Bryan campaigned through Ohio, McKinley again called on Depew to follow him, and the sixty-two-year-old capi-

talist, one of the wittiest men of his day, successfully trailed the youthful Democrat.

A troupe of ancient Civil War generals—Dan Sickles, O. O. Howard, Russell Alger, Thomas Stewart, George Warden—roamed the Middle West in General Alger's private car, trailing a flatcar on which a cannon was mounted. Known as the "Patriotic Heroes' Battalion," they visited 210 towns and travelled six thousand miles in the cause of McKinley. William Beer, a political agent for the New York Life Insurance Company, was made ringmaster and lived a nightmare of listening to old battles rehashed, hunting for bourbon and liver pills, and keeping track of Sickles' wooden leg. But it was an education, too. At one junction in Illinois, young Mr. Beer couldn't understand why the crowd was strangely cool to Sickles until he was informed that this was "a blue Presbyterian district" where folks did not take kindly to a man who had shot his wife's lover. Manager Beer quickly gave his audience O. O. Howard, "the Christian soldier."

The Bureau of Publication and Printing, run by Perry S. Heath of the Cincinnati *Commercial Gazette,* was the heart of Hanna's "campaign of education." It distributed 200 million pieces of literature—an average of fourteen for each voter! And the Republican Congressional Committee in Washington issued another 50 million, mostly reprints of speeches by congressmen and senators. Republican literature came in twelve languages besides English—German, Italian, French, Spanish, Danish, Norwegian, Swedish, Polish, Dutch, Hungarian, Hebrew, and modern Greek. More than 275 different documents were printed, ranging in size from a 456-page *Campaign Textbook* to an editorial from the Emporia, Kansas, *Gazette.* When John Ireland, the Roman Catholic Archbishop of St. Paul, attacked Bryan and his "socialistic" proposals, the Republicans gleefully distributed 250,000 copies of his statement. (The Democrats countered by printing a million copies of a pamphlet by the Archbishop of Dublin that suggested that the Irish land problems had been caused by hard money.)

Charles Dick, who acted as Republican go-between with the nation's notions manufacturers, approving new designs and placing orders, saw to it that the electorate was well supplied with buttons, ribbons, banners, five-color lithographs of the dark-eyed candidate in solemn pose, and an assortment of "funny money," such as the phony silver dollar that bore a caricature of Bryan with the inscription, IN GOD WE TRUST . . . FOR THE OTHER 47 CENTS. (The effect of a silver standard would have been something like a fifty per cent devaluation of the dollar.)

The Republican National Committee also distributed press releases and "boilerplate" mats to country newspapers with a combined circulation of five million. In rare instances newspapers were subsidized directly, but the more standard practice was to place large orders, such as the standing order for 35,000 copies of the Canton *Repository*, which was owned by Mrs. McKinley's family. It was hardly necessary to bribe editors and publishers, however, for never had they been so unanimous as in support of McKinley. Bryan even managed to unite such bitter rivals as *Puck* and *Judge* in opposition to him. The *Nation*, which in March had written that McKinley possessed the most "shut-in mental horizon" since William Henry Harrison, now wrote that "the question . . . is one of means to an end—the end being to keep votes away from Bryan." Every major magazine except the *Arena*, edited by B. O. Flower, opposed free silver. The Democrats had no press support at all in Chicago and Baltimore. In Boston the only Bryan paper, the *Evening Dispatch*, folded two weeks before the election as advertisers preferred to tout their wares in what they considered organs of more respectable opinion. Even some of the major southern papers, such as the Charleston *News and Courier*, the New Orleans *Picayune*, and the Richmond *Times*, refused to endorse the Democratic ticket. Press treatment of Bryan was often rough, but only the *New York Times* questioned his sanity.

The pulpit became a popular place to damn Bryan and free silver. Cheap money was clearly immoral: did not the commandment say, "Thou shalt not steal"? The Reverend Cortland Myers of the Brooklyn Baptist Temple told his congregants on a Sunday morning in mid-September that the Democratic platform was made in hell.

Employers were less subtle. "The Harlan and Hollingsworth Company of this city have received a contract for a boat costing $300,000," wrote the Wilmington *Morning News* on November 3. "One clause in the contract provided that in the event of Bryan's election the contract shall be cancelled. If the boat is built here $160,000 of its cost would be paid to Wilmington workmen for wages." Notes in pay envelopes, lectures by shop foremen, and placards in the plants advised on the most judicious manner to cast the ballot. The head of the Steinway piano works was reported to have said, "Men, vote as you please, but if Bryan is elected tomorrow the whistle will not blow Wednesday morning." A Standard Oil executive went one step further by transferring fifty Democratic workers from the Findlay refinery to Lima and fifty from Lima to Findlay; thus all one hundred failed to meet residence requirements and were disenfranchised. Hanna was not behind the campaign, but he could hardly have been unaware of its existence.

Some Democrats thought that such tactics would boomerang, but old Senator Teller shook his head, "Boys, I'm afraid it beats us. If I were a working man and had nothing but my job, I am afraid when I came to vote I would think of Molly and the babies."

Hanna left little to chance as he divided the electorate into voting blocs, assigning a staff and a budget to each, so that within the Republican National Committee there were divisions for women (who had been given the vote only in Colorado, Wyoming, and Utah), Negroes, Germans, travelling salesmen, even bicyclists ("wheelmen"). Key states in the Middle West were polled again and again to determine changes in public opinion. What the pollsters missed was undoubtedly picked up by Hanna's spies at Democratic headquarters. Dawes was put in charge of the important Chicago office and promptly instituted competitive bidding, central purchasing, and strict audits. A careful observer estimated that before Hanna's time forty per cent of all campaign contributions were wasted; Hanna trimmed the waste to fifteen or twenty per cent. Hanna, the businessman-politician, was the first to bring some semblance of order to the technical management of presidential campaigning. It was his contribution to the art of American politics.

What did the Republican campaign cost? Some have placed the tab as high as $16.5 million. Immediately after the election Dawes prepared a careful financial statement which came out to $3,562,325.59.

Dawes's total was twice what had been spent in 1892. (It cost $200,000 to run for President in 1864 and $500,000 in 1872.) But Dawes's tabulation—and there is no reason to question it—is only half the story. Other organizations spent freely—the Gold Democrats, the Republican Congressional Committee, state and local committees. The American Protective Tariff League in New York paid for distribution of twenty million pieces of Republican campaign literature. Others contributed in services rather than cash—complimentary use of Western Union wires, railroad passes for McKinley speakers, special fares to Canton, the use of corporation employees. Altogether, the cost of running William McKinley for President probably came to between six and seven million dollars. The Republicans must have outspent the Democrats by six or seven to one.

As election day approached, Hanna had only one worry: that he had pushed his preparations too hard, that his troops were too enthusiastic too early. So on the last Saturday, October 31, he called for a national celebration that would climax the campaign by making "patriotism" and "McKinley" synonymous. There were marches in San Francisco and Chicago. Along New York's Fifth Avenue over 750,000 people cheered as the Business Men's Sound Money Association led an estimated one hundred thousand paraders, waving flags, wearing the emblematic color of the cause—gold. From 10 A.M. to 6 P.M. they locked step, shouting in cadence, "Left, left, Bryan will get left."

Bands started to play at six o'clock on election day morning in Canton. By nine, McKinley appeared on his front porch—it was shaky now after the stresses of the past months—and walked to his polling place, where he got in line behind a mechanic in working clothes. Bryan was in Omaha. He woke at 6:30, ate a beefsteak, an omelette, and potatoes, and boarded the train for Lincoln, where he voted at the firehouse in a room with tethered horses. Toward evening the people began to gather in front of newspaper offices. In large cities the returns were flashed on a screen by means of "magic lanterns." As the figures began to indicate a McKinley victory, the men at the factories in the winner's home town tied down the levers of the steam whistles. Bryan, at home, wearing a black velvet jacket, a pink carnation in his buttonhole, looked to a reporter like "a general reading the reports of some great battle in which whole armies were swept away." McKinley received 7,035,638 votes; Bryan, 6,467,946. The electoral vote was more decisively Republican, 271 to 176. It was not a landslide, but McKinley's margin was the most substantial of any Republican's since 1872.

Bryan lost because he was not able to penetrate the urban labor vote. As predicted, McKinley swept the East while Bryan carried all of the South; McKinley did better in the West than expected, but the election was decided—as planned—in the five crucial states of the Old Northwest—Ohio, Indiana, Illinois, Wisconsin, Michigan. All went Republican. The President-elect knelt in prayer beside his mother's bed. The old lady asked: "Oh, God, keep him humble." In an exclusive Chicago club, long after midnight, some of the nation's great merchants and bankers played "Follow the Leader," under sofas, chairs, tables, upstairs, downstairs, laughing, shouting, dancing in each other's arms. Mark Hanna played whist at the Union Club in Cleveland. "He had made a President and he had done it visibly," wrote historian Thomas Beer. "It is hard to forgive such realism." When the trend was conclusive, Hanna went over to the Central Armory to greet the party faithful. He then sent a wire to his candidate: GOD'S IN HIS HEAVEN, ALL'S RIGHT WITH THE WORLD.

Stephen Hess of Washington, D.C., is the author of America's Political Dynasties: From Adams to Kennedy, *recently published by Doubleday.*

Morgan to the Rescue CONTINUED FROM PAGE 63

not be sold abroad, Morgan's cable predicted that the arrangement "will be most creditable all parties and pay good profit." He also implied—perhaps craftily—that there was serious competition for the assignment ("should dislike see business largely hands Speyer and Co. and similar houses, who more sanguine European loans than your cables indicate") and that the syndicates' motivating factor would be sheer self-interest. ("We all have large interests dependent upon maintenance sound currency.") "There are always two reasons a man does something," Morgan once said in another connection. "The good one he gives—and the real one." Which was his real motive in this case—patriotism or profit—would be endlessly debated in years to come.

Curtis telephoned Friday afternoon that the Washington reaction was favorable, and Morgan began firing off more cables setting in motion the complex international machinery required to draw in the necessary gold. He met with Curtis at his home that midnight and again the next morning at the Subtreasury, where the panic was beginning to subside. The three million dollars in total Treasury withdrawals on Friday and Saturday were far outbalanced by nine million dollars' worth of gold that was taken off ships in the harbor and turned back to the Treasury.

Morgan insisted afterward that at the first Subtreasury conference there had been no discussion of the amount of interest to be paid on the new bonds. ("It was not really a question of price. It was a question of success.") The 1894 bonds had paid 3 per cent. The newspapers were now printing the rumor that the new issue would pay 3½. Now, on Saturday morning, Morgan told Curtis that the price would have to be 3¾ per cent. Both he and Curtis assumed this would be acceptable, and the Treasury man agreed to call Morgan at three on Sunday afternoon with the final go-ahead signal. Sunday evening in the Morgan household was regularly given over to family hymn-singing, but it is not known whether or not the banker was available that night to sing his favorite, "O Zion, Haste, Thy Mission High Fulfilling." Curtis had called at the appointed time, but only with the unsettling news that a messenger with an explanatory letter would arrive on the morning train. "The public and press believe the negotiation practically completed. . . . Effect of abandonment upon all interests would now be worse than if never begun," read Morgan's cable to London.

The Treasury letter, delivered to him before breakfast on Monday, rejected his solution for the gold problem and informed him that a public sale of the new bond issue would be announced that afternoon. The Democratic press had spent the weekend denouncing the secret nature of the negotiations ("dark lantern financiering") and was plumping for a 3 per cent loan. ("If the banks won't take it, the people will," insisted the New York *World*.) Cleveland, perhaps unduly encouraged by the halt in the gold run, had taken another look at the political consequences of the private deal and had pulled back.

Morgan detested telephones, in the Nineties still unreliable and highly public instruments, but now he did not hesitate. Much of his morning was spent on the long-distance lines talking to Curtis, who finally got Carlisle to delay the announcement of the public sale for a day. He had sent Belmont to the capital on the ten o'clock train, Morgan told Curtis, and he himself would leave at once. They would talk to the President. There was no other way. In midafternoon Morgan took the ferry to Jersey City and boarded his private car, which was then attached to the Congressional Limited. He brought with him his junior partner, Robert Bacon (later Theodore Roosevelt's Secretary of State), and his lawyer, Francis Lynde Stetson, who was expected to be especially useful since he had been a law partner of Cleveland's in the interval between presidential terms.

When Morgan's train arrived in Washington, about a dozen newspapermen and Daniel Lamont were waiting on the platform. Lamont, a former reporter himself, was on the government roster as Secretary of War, but was more active as Cleveland's trouble shooter. (Mark Hanna described the War Department in the mid-Nineties as the only Cabinet seat for which a busy man could spare the time from his own affairs.) Lamont told Morgan that the President would not see him, and then visibly braced himself. When angry, Morgan was an alarming sight. Not only would his eyes seem to start out of his big head, but his great, bulbous red nose, the result of an affliction called *acne rosacea*, would, as Lincoln Steffens later remembered it, "flash and darken, flash and darken." He glared down now at Lamont. "I have come to Washington to see the President, and I am going to stay until I see him," he said in a booming voice and stomped off in the snow toward the cab stand. He shook off the press by directing the cab not to the Arlington, where he always stayed, but to the home of a woman friend on K Street.

The unbidden visitor, publicly rebuffed, was no longer standing on ceremony. Stetson was dispatched to the White House to invade Cleveland's quarters and persuade him to change his mind. He got no further than the front door, but about ten o'clock Bacon called to say that Attorney General Richard Olney was willing to talk to Morgan. Olney had heard from Carlisle the alarming report that one gold draft for over twelve million dollars might be presented at the New York Subtreasury the next day, and after conferring with Morgan, agreed to urge the President to see the banker and his friends. Having done everything he could, Morgan went on to the Arlington, where he avoided the inevitable press reception by ducking in the ladies' entrance on H Street. At midnight he sent his younger colleagues off to bed. As usual, he had brought with him from New York a small mahogany folding table and the silver box holding his solitaire cards. The game he played for the next several hours was "Miss Milligan," a solitaire variation involving two decks of cards and a maneuver called "waiving," which allows a single obstructing card to be temporarily lifted out of the tableau when a game is hopelessly blocked. "By this privilege," notes one solitaire manual, "many desperate conditions can be remedied." The telephone call Morgan was waiting for had not come at four o'clock, and soon afterward he went to bed.

Saying very little, the four New Yorkers breakfasted later that morning in Morgan's sitting room. Bacon had just hung up the telephone after hearing the New York office prediction of a renewed run on the gold reserve and Morgan had pulled out his first cigar of the day, when Olney called to say that the President would meet with them. Without stopping to light up, Morgan called for his hat and coat, and with Belmont and the two Morgan aides falling in behind him, strode out into the bitter February wind and across Lafayette Square to the White House. Carlisle and Olney had already joined the President in his cluttered office in the East Wing. All three of them were heavy-eyed from lack of sleep. Curtis was not on hand. His letter, sent early that morning to Carlisle, suggesting that the gap between the proposed interest rates "is nothing compared with panic and suspension," had not gone down well.

Cleveland was not smoking, so Morgan held his cigar unlit in his hand. Although the two men were social acquaintances, there was no small talk. The President brusquely announced that there had been no change in his views: the public bond sale would go on. Having at last reached the official wheelhouse of the nation, however, Morgan did not propose to leave. Apparently without specific encouragement from the President, he and his colleagues took up inconspicuous positions in a corner of the room. During the next three hours they sat, watching and waiting, while clerks shuffled in and out, Carlisle and Cleveland discussed details of the new bond issue and passed papers back and forth, and the telephone rang constantly in the room across the hall, bringing the latest reports of new drafts on the Treasury. At one point Cleveland left the office and was gone for nearly an hour. Meanwhile Morgan sat on the sidelines, unheeded and powerless, "like a messenger waiting for an answer," as his son-in-law later described it, adding, "it was not a situation he was used to." At last, about noon, Carlisle read aloud from a yellow slip of paper a message just received from the telephone room. Only nine million dollars in gold coin remained in the New York Subtreasury. (There were only a few gold *coins* in other repositories, and the bullion holdings were everywhere at an all-time low.) From his corner Morgan broke his silence.

"The Secretary of the Treasury knows of one draft for twelve million. If that's presented today, it's all over," he said.

Cleveland put down the papers he was holding and sat back in his chair. "Have you any suggestions, Mr. Morgan?" he asked. It was surrender. At this moment the President of the United States, noted Lewis Corey in *The House of Morgan*, was like a small businessman who, after a long struggle, is finally compelled by economic necessity to yield to the overwhelming power of the giant combine. "Independent, belligerent, stubborn," he was "yet cannily accepting the inevitable."

Morgan leaned forward and talked fast. He went over once more the details of his proposition, defending the high interest rate as necessary to attract gold from abroad and bring it out of protective custody in this country. In private communications to his partners he had said that 3⅝ per cent would make the undertaking worthwhile, but apparently none of the men in the President's office pressed him to compromise. As for the problem that Congress clearly would not authorize such a private arrangement, he cited a legal basis for the transaction. During a Civil War emergency, Congress had passed a law covering the matter, he told the group, and it could be found in the Revised Statutes. Olney was sent to fetch the proper volume and came back with it open to an 1862 law providing that "the Secretary of the Treasury may purchase coin with any of the bonds or notes of the United States ... at such rates and upon such terms as he may deem most advantageous to the public interest." In later years Morgan often mentioned that the recollection of this law had come to him during his long hours of Miss Milligan the night before. In fact, it was probably

Curtis who had come upon the statute some weeks earlier and had described it to both Carlisle and Morgan. But then, as Stillman had noted, Morgan was a poet.

A little over sixty million dollars would restore the Treasury reserve to the sanctified hundred million. The contract therefore specified that the syndicates would provide the government with 3,500,000 ounces of gold, which would be paid for with $62,315,400 worth of 4 per cent, thirty-year bonds (sold to the syndicates at 104½). At this modest premium, the actual interest rate came down to 3¾ per cent. The bond sale differed from those of 1894 in that it was a private contract, that it cost the syndicates less (the price of the earlier bonds had been 117), and that the syndicate guaranteed that at least half of the gold would come from abroad. Before the meeting broke up Cleveland exacted a further promise.

"What guarantee have we that if we adopt this plan, gold will not continue to be shipped abroad and while we are getting it in, it will go out, so that we will not reach our goal?" he asked Morgan. "Will you guarantee this will not happen?"

"Yes, sir," said Morgan instantly, without consulting Belmont or anyone else. "I will guarantee it during the life of the syndicate ... until the goal has been reached."

It was now after two o'clock. As the bankers rose to leave, someone noticed there was brown dust all over Morgan's trousers and on the carpet at his feet. In the tense moments of the long morning he had crushed to powder the cigar he had brought into the room unlighted so many hours before.

There is no doubt the little company of men in the President's office that day sincerely believed that, as Morgan was soon cabling his London partners, the nation had been saved from "dangers ... so great scarcely anyone dare whisper them." They could not have been so naïve as to expect congratulations all around, but they may not have been prepared for the ferociousness of some of the attacks that followed publication of the bond-sale terms. A senator from Alabama described Morgan and Belmont as having first crippled the government and then moved in to strangle it. The New York *World* denounced them as "bloodsucking Jews and aliens," pointing out that the name "Belmont" had originally been Schönberg. And before condemning the contract on the floor of the

House, Bryan had the clerk read aloud Shylock's bond, the infamous "pound-of-flesh" contract in *The Merchant of Venice*. Meanwhile Morgan set about drawing in gold. "You can ship any gold you choose," he cabled London, "bar gold, sovereigns, U.S. gold coin, napoleons...."

As a mark of his return to favor, it was announced that Curtis would be treated to a free ocean voyage to deliver the European consignment of bonds overseas. The level in the Treasury vaults rose steadily, although the silverite bloc had sullenly prevented the exercise of a clause in the contract that reduced the interest to 3 per cent if Congress made the bonds specifically payable in gold, a vote that cost the government sixteen million dollars in interest. By March the bonds the syndicates had been allowed to buy at 104½ were selling for 117, and in June they hit 124.

The goldbugs credited this rise to restored public confidence as the Treasury reserve grew and to the power of the Morgan-Belmont endorsement. The silverites called it proof that the bonds could have been sold without the government's resorting to the expensive and humiliating private arrangement and estimated the joint syndicate's profit at as high as sixteen million dollars. The rumor even spread, on no evidence whatever, that a cut of this profit had gone to Cleveland. Tales of outrageous returns to the syndicate were hardly quieted when, during the inevitable congressional investigation the following year, Morgan said the money he had made on the deal was his business. However, the syndicate book at the Morgan offices in New York showed the profit of the American half of the operation to be just over two million dollars. Of the thirty-one million dollars in bonds allotted to the sixty-one syndicate members, the Morgan and Belmont companies each took a little over a quarter of a million dollars' worth. The Morgan firm's profit, including interest and half of the American syndicate managers' commission, came to $295,652.93. Since the profit from the European operation was smaller, the Morgan company's combined New York and London return was about half a million dollars, or, as Morgan could have pointed out, perhaps half the amount it might collect for straightening out the financial affairs of a minor New England railroad.

The syndicate report takes no account of the expenses of keeping Morgan's promise to Cleveland to protect the Treasury against gold withdrawals and exports. Morgan managed this feat by involving in the enterprise all the country's major banks and investment houses with European connections, inviting them to join the syndicate and share the profits and in return exacting their temporary agreement not to draw gold out of the Treasury or to ship it abroad. To assure their compliance Morgan succeeded in controlling the natural fluctuations of the international exchange rate by such measures as buying notes in New York and selling them in London at a loss to his own firm. Part of his convolute strategy required him to keep the gold reserve below ninety million during the spring months, which he did by holding gold certificates in his pocket ready for presentation at the Treasury any time it moved above this sum. Virtually no gold left the country between February and mid-June, 1895, when he permitted the reserve to rise to $107,000,000. "We see the curious spectacle," wrote Curtis in a letter home, "of the United States finances being controlled by a committee of which J. P. Morgan is chairman . . . while the Secretary of the Treasury sits practically powerless in his office." During the congressional investigation in 1896, Morgan was asked why he was so determined to keep other firms from entering the negotiations to bring in the gold and see that it stayed. "It would only have made for competition," he said. "And besides, *they could not do it.*"

Before the great bond crisis Morgan was little known outside eastern banking and railroad circles. After it, to the end of his life, his was the name that led the roll of the "insolent money oligarchy" that it became more and more fashionable to denounce. There is no evidence that this bothered him in the slightest. For allowing "Wall Streeters and their gold to roam the administration like panthers in their native jungles," as one western newspaper described it, Grover Cleveland suffered more than name-calling. By stubbornly choosing what he believed to be the good of the nation over party unity, he surrendered his influence in Democratic politics and was condemned to sit helplessly by at the 1896 convention as his party, taken over by the silverites, declared total war on the "cross of gold." Their defeat that November brought about not only the end of the free-silver movement but the eclipse of the Democratic party for half a generation.

The United States went formally on the gold standard in 1900 and left it in 1933. World War I had unsettled all national monetary systems, and by the 1930's the idea of reckoning a nation's honor and credit solely on the basis of its store of precious metal had a nineteenth-century look. Some of the silverites' arguments, particularly those favoring an increase in the amount of money in circulation, were beginning to appear less addleheaded. And as government philosophies change, so, it seems, do those of great banking houses. When Franklin Roosevelt announced that the country was abandoning the gold standard, the only important Wall Street firm to support the move was the House of Morgan.

Andy Logan is a member of the staff of The New Yorker *and the author of* The Man Who Robbed the Robber Barons, *a biography of Colonel William D'Alton Mann, publisher of* Town Topics, *a blackmailing scandal sheet that received clandestine financial support from most of the tycoons of the 1890's, including Pierpont Morgan.*

Good News for Detroit

There will, first of all, be the motor truck for heavy traffic. . . . And sooner or later, no doubt, the numerous advantages of such an arrangement will lead to the organization of large carrier companies, using such motor trucks to carry goods in bulk or parcels on the high roads.

In the next place, and parallel with the motor truck, there will develop the hired or privately owned motor carriage. . . . It will be capable of a day's journey of three hundred miles or more. One will change nothing—unless it is the driver—from stage to stage. One will be free to dine where one chooses, hurry when one chooses, travel asleep or awake, stop and pick flowers, turn over in bed of a morning and tell the carriage to wait—unless one sleeps aboard.

And, thirdly, there will be the motor omnibus, developing out of the horse omnibus. . . .

Parkways in Utopia

[The] roads will be very different . . . they will be used only by soft-tired conveyances; the battering horseshoes, the perpetual filth of horse traffic, and the clumsy wheels of laden carts will never wear them. It may be that they will have a surface like that of some cycle-racing tracks, though since they will be open to wind and weather, it is perhaps more probable they will be made of very good asphalt sloped to drain, and still more probable that they will be of some new substance altogether. . . . Their traffic in opposite directions will probably be strictly separated.

Change for the Railways

And it may be that many railways, which are neither capable of modification into suburban motor tracks, nor of development into luxurious through routes, will find, in spite of the loss of many elements of their old activity, that there is still a profit to be made from a certain section of the heavy goods traffic, and from cheap excursions. There are forms of work for which railways seem to be particularly

The Nineties Look to the Future

By H. G. WELLS

As the nineteenth century died with the year 1900 and the twentieth sprang to life with 1901, George Brinton Harvey, the editor of the distinguished monthly the North American Review, *asked H. G. Wells to write six essays predicting what the new century would be like. Wells, then only thirty-four, already had a reputation as a seer; he had published his science-fiction novel* The Time Machine, *as well as* The Invisible Man *and* The War of the Worlds. *(Max Beerbohm caricatured Wells's prophetic pose in the drawing above, titled "Mr. H. G. Wells, prophet and idealist, conjuring up the darling Future.") In his essays for the* North American Review *Wells touched upon subjects as far-ranging as war, the twentieth-century house, and automobiles. These selections prove that his seer's eye saw well.*

adapted, and which the diversion of a great portion of their passenger traffic would enable them to conduct even more efficiently. . . .

Almost certainly the existing lines of railway will develop and differentiate, some in one direction and some in another, according to the nature of the pressure upon them. Almost all will probably be still in existence and in divers ways busy a hundred years from now.

Megalopolis

We are on the eve of a great development of centrifugal possibilities. And since it has been shown that a city of pedestrians is inexorably limited by a radius of about four miles, and that a horse-using city may grow out to seven or eight, it follows that the available area of a city which can offer a cheap suburban journey of thirty miles an hour is a circle with a radius of thirty miles. . . . But thirty miles is only a very moderate estimate of speed, and the available area for the social equivalent of the favored season-ticket holders of to-day will have a radius of over one hundred miles, and be almost equal to the area of Ireland. The radius that will sweep the area available for such as now live in the outer suburbs will include a still vaster area. Indeed, it is not too much to say that the vast stretch of country from Washington to Albany will be all of it "available" to the active citizen of New York and Philadelphia. . . .

Live Better Electrically

[The family of the future] will probably not keep a servant for two very excellent reasons—because, in the first place, they will not want one, and, in the second, they will not get one, if they do. . . . The great proportion of the servant's duties consists merely in drudgery that the stupidities of our present-day method of house construction entail, and which the more sanely constructed house of the future will avoid. . . . It is the lack of proper warming appliances which necessitates a vast amount of coal carrying and dirt distribution, and it is this dirt, mainly, that has so painfully to be removed again. The house of the future will probably be warmed in its walls from some power-generating station, as, indeed, already very many houses are lit at the present day.... [Or] take now the bedroom work. The lack of ingenuity in sanitary fittings at present forbids the obvious convenience of hot and cold water supply to the bedroom, and there is a mighty fetching and carrying of water and slops to be got through daily; but all that will cease. Every bedroom will have its own bath-dressing room.... Downstairs, a vast amount of needless labor at present arises out of table ware. "Washing up" consists of a tedious cleansing and wiping of each table utensil in turn, whereas it should be possible to immerse all dirty table ware in a suitable solvent for a few minutes, and then run that off for the articles to dry.... There remains the cooking. To-day, cooking with its incidentals is a very serious business; the coaling, the ashes, the horrible moments of heat, the hot, black things to handle, the silly, vague recipes, the want of neat apparatus, and the want of intelligence to demand or use neat apparatus. One always imagines a cook working with a crimsoned face and bare, blackened arms. But with a neat little range, heated by electricity, and provided with thermometer, with absolutely controllable temperatures and proper heat screens, cooking might very easily be made a pleasant amusement for intelligent invalid ladies.

The Plural Society

...For one Morality, there will be many moralities. Each human being will, in the face of circumstances, work out his or her particular early training as his or her character determines. And, although there will be a general convention upon which the most diverse people will meet, it will only be with persons who have come to identical or similar conclusions in the matter of moral conduct...that really frequent and intimate intercourse will go on. In other words, there will be a process of moral segregation set up.... And these segregations...will probably round off and complete themselves at last as distinct and separate cultures.

As the moral ideas realize themselves in *ménage* and habits, so the ideals will seek to find expression in a literature, and the passive drifting together will pass ever into a phase of more or less conscious and intentional organization. The segregating groups will develop fashions of costume, types of manners and bearing.... Life is already most wonderfully arbitrary and experimental, and for the coming century this must be its essential social history, a great drifting and unrest of people, a shifting and regrouping and breaking up again of groups, great multitudes seeking to find themselves.

Support for Billy Mitchell

The revolution that is in progress from the old war to a new war different in its entire nature from the old is marked, primarily, by the steady progress in range and efficiency of the rifle and of the field gun—more particularly of the rifle.... One can conceive it as provided in the future with crossthread, telescopic sights.... It will probably also take on some of the characters of the machine gun.... Between contiguous nations that have mastered the art of war, instead of the pouring clouds of cavalry of the old dispensation, this will be the opening phase of the struggle, a vast duel all along the frontier between groups of skilled marksmen, continually being relieved and refreshened from the rear.... For eight miles on either side of the firing lines—whose fire will probably never altogether die away while the war lasts—men will live and eat and sleep under the imminence of unanticipated death. Such will be the opening phase of the war that is speedily to come.

And behind the thin firing line on either side, a vast multitude of people will be at work. Indeed, the whole mass of the efficients in the state will have to be at work....

...The game will be largely to crowd and crumple the line, to stretch it over an arc to the breaking point, to secure a position from which to shell and destroy its supports and provisions, and to capture or destroy its guns....

...Few people, I fancy, who know the work of Langley, Lilienthal, Pilcher, Maxim and Chanute, but will be inclined to believe that long before the year 2000 A.D., probably before 1950, a successful aeroplane will have soared and come home safe and sound. Directly that is accomplished, the new invention will be most assuredly applied to war. This opening phase, therefore, of deadlocked lines of marksmen below will be accompanied by a desperate and finally decisive struggle for the command of the sky.... The victor in that aerial struggle will tower with pitilessly watchful eyes over his adversary, will concentrate his guns and all his strength unobserved, will mark all his adversary's roads and communications and sweep them with sudden...disasters of shot and shell.

Rue Britannia

The United States of America are rapidly taking, or have already taken, the ascendency in the iron and steel and electrical industries out of the hands of the British, they are developing a far ampler and more thorough system of higher scientific education than the British.... These things render the transfer of the present mercantile and naval ascendency of Great Britain to the United States during the next two or three decades a very probable thing....

Cheer for U Thant

The suggestion is powerful, the conclusion is hard to resist, that, through whatever disorders of danger and conflict, whatever centuries of misunderstanding and bloodshed, men may still have to pass, [mankind] will finally attain to the establishment of one world state...The nations and boundaries of to-day do no more than mark claims to exemptions, privileges and corners in the market.... Against all these old isolations, these obsolescent particularisms, the forces of mechanical and scientific development fight and fight irresistibly; and upon the general recognition of this conflict, upon the intelligence and courage with which its inflexible conditions are negotiated, depends very largely the amount of bloodshed and avoidable misery the coming years will hold.

Charles Dana Gibson's caption for this drawing was very simple: WHO CARES? And it is, perhaps, a good idea to remind ourselves—after all the portentous matters discussed earlier in this volume—that some splendid things never change; the way of an eagle on a rock, the way of a man with a maid. These people don't know that they are late-Victorian, mid-imperialistic, and about to become Edwardian. They don't care about hemlines or collars, or trends that historians will later carve into fine, delicate pieces. Neither realism nor romanticism, neither pragmatism nor idealism, neither faith-to-go nor Freud-to-come even enter their minds; they are simply slogging through the joys and sorrows of life with the rest of us without caring a fig about the "period" they live in. In fact, they don't even know it is raining.